Who Cares

A Loving Guide for My Future Caregivers

Updated Edition

*Providing future caregivers the most important facts about **your** life*

Dee Marrella

PRESS

A Division of the Diogenes Consortium

SANFORD · FLORIDA

This guide is intended as a means for the user to create a journal of their life's events and to share personal thoughts with its readers. before taking any action that could have legal ramifications, discuss such matters with an attorney of your choice. Likewise, before taking any action effecting your health care, discuss those actions with your personal physicians.

Published by DC Press
2445 River Tree Circle
Sanford, FL 32771
http://www.focusonethics.com

This book was set in Adobe Novarese
Cover Design and Composition by Jonathan Pennell

Library of Congress Catalog Number: 2004103880
          Marrella. Dee,
Who Cares, A Loving Guide for My Future Caregivers |Updated Edition|
          ISBN: 1-932021-12-4

First DC Press Edition
10   9   8   7   6   5   4   3   2   1
Printed in the United States of America

This book is lovingly dedicated
to my mother, Beatrice Delia —
A happy person who suffered so much
in her later years.

To my sisters,
Terry Nicoletti and Karen Wiesen —
Together, we tried our very best.

To my daughters, Tammy Toso,
Lani Martin and Robin Russo —
Your love and support during a very
trying time will never be forgotten.

To the love of my life, Len —
You encouraged me to care for my
Mom. You shared my stress and pain.
For this I am forever grateful.

To the older generation —
You taught me so many of life's most
important lessons.

Sympathy sees and says, "I'm sorry."

Compassion sees and says, "I'll help."

—Anonymous

CONTENTS

Part I: General Instructions

Part II: Priorities for Care
Medical Information

Part III: My Preferences

Part IV: Who Am I?

Part V: Relationships

Part VI: Holiday and Religious Observance

Part VII: Important Names

Part VIII: FInancial and Business Affairs

Part IX:Life's Lessons

Part X: Words & Phrases to Keep Handy

Part XI: Notes

About the Author

PREFACE

How I came to write this guide.

OR A YEAR AND A HALF I had been visiting my 93-year-old mother in a nursing home. Never did I think I would have to face the heartbreak and guilt of seeing my Mom helpless and in a wheelchair. Nor was I prepared for the heartbreak I would feel for those around her.

Some sights will never leave me:

- A woman sitting in the hallway, purse in hand, never moving from her particular chair, waiting for someone to come for her — all day, every day, for months.

- A handsome man in his eighties — father of twelve children — eagerly waiting for the Christmas holidays, hoping to see any of his children. Not one showed up...not until his death a few weeks later. (Was his heart broken?)

- A short, humped-back, older woman constantly walking the halls all alone — never talking to anyone, never visited. When she sat near other residents, she was chased away. As she walked passed, she was taunted. She just kept walking.

- A lovely lady in her fifties who came to visit her mother — a victim of Alzheimer's. Sometimes she looked so tired, just coming from her own job. She had a brother, but he never visited his mother. He rationalized that his mother had actually died years earlier. (I wondered — if he suffered from the same disease — would his mother have come to visit him? I'm sure she would have gone every day possible to lovingly care for him.)

I could go on with such stories. There is heartbreak on both sides. Parents are getting older and more helpless. Children are trying to cope with the worry, exhaustion and guilt.

I loved my mother very much. My mother loved me very much. I know there are many of you who feel the same — you love your parents, you love your children. Sitting at the nursing home, observing all of these things, I saw how quickly the years can overtake us, how little time might be left before we become "the older generation" — the ones in need of caregivers.

If I have my wish, my children will not have to face the worry and heartache I felt as a caregiver for my mother. I do not want them to be overwhelmed or to feel any guilt about my care, my contentment, or my happiness. When I asked myself what I could do to make it a little easier for my children — when I reach my later years and possibly become helpless, I realized that there were a lot of questions that could be answered in advance. There were so many questions that I would like to have asked my mother. But that was never to be. It was too late for that. When I was ready to ask the questions, she was no longer able to answer them. She had become forgetful and communication was tough. Roles reversed. She became the child and her children were making all of her decisions for her.

I had not lived in my mother's home for many years. What were her fears? What were her opinions regarding her own health care? What decisions would she have made? What things would give her joy? These questions and others have led me to write this guide. If I cannot leave my children anything else, I do want to leave them **less guilt** and **more peace of mind**. By filling out this book, they will know what my wishes are. They will know what my decisions would be. Besides helping my caregivers I will still have control over my own destiny.

There are little things you might not have told you own family — things that are peculiar to you alone. I was thrilled when my mother turned to me and smiled at something I did to make her a bit more comfortable — and therefore a bit happier. I always felt, however, that there was more that I could have done — if only I had asked her ahead of time. Maybe, if she had left a book like this for her children, my sisters and I would have lived with less guilt and stress.

It is too late for my mother. But it is not too late for my children. I am writing this book for them, and I am writing it for all other individuals who want to help guide their future caregivers and anyone else who cares.

FOREWORD

*E*ARLIER THIS YEAR, after 45 years of marriage, my wife Alice succumbed to the complications of dementia. This condition comes with many different manifestations and I feel fortunate that Alice never experienced elder rages and remained sweet natured throughout her long journey and then died without pain, fear or anxiety. In the months that followed, I discovered Dee Marrella's book **Who Cares** and promptly filled in the blanks with the aid of my granddaughter also named Alice. In the process we both experienced a new understanding.

Dementia is a devastating illness that all people dread and fear as they approach their later years of life. No one wishes to become a burden on his or her family and friends who necessarily will become their caregivers. Watching a loved one slowly disappear brings a profound and prolonged grief, and with it comes uncertainty about whether you are following their wishes and making the correct decisions. In the end, the caregivers suffer as much as the person who is afflicted with the disease.

In this well thought out book, Dee Marrella has provided a great service. It is a concise, yet thorough, roadmap for those who will care for us should we become unable to manage our own affairs and well-being responsibility. While we are of sound mind, it is important to take the time to answer the questions so clearly outlined in this book. It will certainly make the job of "those who care" much easier.

It is difficult to face end-of-life issues squarely and yet it is our responsibility. This book gives us the tools and completing it is an act of love for those who follow.

— Ashbel G. Gulliver, Jr., M.D.

Department of Obstetrics & Gynecology
Charlotte Hungerford Hospital
Torrington, Connecticut

Loving

Kindness

Compassion...

Begin with me

CAVEAT

Do not assume people know
these things about you.

Do not assume that they
will remember.

TELL THEM!

As Garth Wood wrote in **The Myth of Neurosis:
Overcoming the Illness Excuse**:

"...When the old person gives up his job and his role, his strife and his struggle, he is frequently unable to replace it with something of value. As he does less, his self-respect declines and his confidence in himself fails .... If, *however, the old person has retained his activity and interests, striving day after day to acquire new skills or perfect old ones, constantly fighting to overcome any physical deficiency resulting from the aging process, then his self-respect and self-confidence will increase .... By being interested he becomes interesting and he need never become 'old' in the traditional sense."*

AUTHOR'S
COMMENT

CAREGIVERS need guidelines on how to comfort a loved one. When individuals become our caregivers, they should have *our* guidelines available to them. We all worry about wills, funerals, and leaving finances in order — for **after we die.** This book is focused on lessening pain and stress when we are older, sometimes helpless, but *still alive*!

Therefore, this book has two audiences or sets of possible readers:

🍂 The first set constitutes those of us who recognize that we are, in fact, getting older — and that it is possible that we will one day be older, forgetful, infirm, unable to communicate feelings and desires, and/or ineffective in seeing to it that we get what we need.

🍂 The second set is made up of people who will care for us. If we are lucky, we can predict who those people will be and we can pass this book on to them. If we are lucky, they will be the people who love us — our children, other family members, or very close friends.

This book is designed to be filled out by the individual for whom future care is intended and then handed over to your future caregivers. This book is a person's chance to direct not only the care they will receive, but the "who's, what's, when's where's and how's" of his or her daily life.

By filling this book out, you have more control over your own destiny. You will also have given a great gift to your loved ones — peace of mind.

Maybe it is not comfortable for you to discuss this with your caregivers. Maybe it is not comfortable for them either. Maybe you cannot even tell them you have prepared this book for their use. You can, however, leave it with important papers, on your desk, where you stash your unpaid bills, under your address book, where you keep your car keys or medication. In other words, you can leave it where they are bound to find it when suddenly there is a need to take care of you and handle your affairs. Either way, they will have it and be able to be guided by **your wishes**.

If you are one of the lucky individuals who can discuss your wishes with your future caregivers, this book can help open all kinds of doors. If possible give it to your future caregiver now. Ask them to become familiar with it. Invite them to ask you questions. Invite them to make notes in it. Remember: this is a living document in more ways than one.

The guide is divided into eleven parts. I have made every effort to anticipate all the categories that affect our lives — not merely the big decisions, but all the little things that enhance the quality of each day.

Because this is a tool that I too have been using and filling out for my own children, there are places throughout the book where I have jumped right in and provided you, the reader, with sample answers. These are my answers for *my* children. They are there to give you an idea of the scope or detail you may wish to provide in your own responses to your future caregivers. Your responses will certainly be your own.

At the end of the eleven parts, I have added an extra chapter. To supplement the specific guidlines you provide your caregivers, I offer some general guidance that can help all of our future care-givers.

Following this final chapter, there is a section called "Notes." This contains a grouping of blank pages that I promised earlier. I am sure you will think of categories that I've not included, that apply to you and your own special needs and requests. You might simply need additional space to complete comments from an earlier chapter. Make these pages your very own.

Another addition to the new edition is one I call 'Words and Phrases To Keep Handy.' Here you will find some important terms with which you should be familiar.

And finally, I ask that you consider writing to me and sharing your own thoughts on how the guide can be enhanced. If you have topics that you feel are important and were left out of this edition, I'd appreciate you sharing your ideas with me. Comments from users have been included in this new edition to improve upon this original concept and make the guide as valuable as possible for future generations.

— **Dee Marrella**

You can reach Dee at address supplied on the final page of this book.

PUBLISHER'S COMMENT

*W*hen the first edition of this book was released, no one had any idea of the impact it would have on individuals and families who acquired copies. Letters, faxes, e-mails, and phone calls have poured in from all around North America thanking Dee Marrella for coming up with the concept and for the doors that have been opened as a result of people filling out the pages and becoming proactive in their own future caregiving. As the publisher of **Who Cares: A Loving Guide for My Future**

Caregivers, I want to add my own thanks to Dee for having confidence in DC Press to serve as her publisher. I honestly believe that this new edition will do even more for those who utilize it. It is certainly a work of love and it will always be a work in progress — since something this personal will always be evolving.

As I stated in the first edition, youth gives most of us the false sense that life has no limits with no end in sight. Little time is spent contemplating old age or some future illness or disability. However, by the time mid-life hits us, most people find it all quite shocking. I've often told people that "I went to bed the other night and I was just 18. When I woke up, I wasn't." Time flies by and the years pile up. Before long, we are dealing with challenges we were never educated about and are unprepared to face.

Some who pick up this book may already have been dealing with health-related challenges for some time. The majority will be healthy and perhaps see no reason to even look seriously at the pages of this book. Many will have already seen a parent become incapacitated. That can be a major education. Realizing that caregiving is a full-time occupation, many of us look toward retirement communities, nursing homes, assisted living centers, hospitalization, and/or long-term care arrangements. Many such realities can be a good experience for all concerned; often they are not.

Often this becomes an extremely troubling time. Bodies weaken. Minds that were once sharp as a tack can become incapable of even short-term memory. Even ordinary conversations can be labored. No one can escape the impact.

When an adult child, close relative, good friend, or any non-professional takes on the role of caregiver, the responsibilities can be overwhelming. For those who have never had any training, the challenges can seem insurmountable. The process of caring for someone who was once perhaps your own source of strength can seem surreal. Cost can be an issue. But even if it isn't, money cannot guarantee that the caregiving experience will be smooth and event free.

Regardless of caregiving being personalized or institutionalized, it is possible for any of us who allows ourselves to look into the future to help those who will eventually become our caregivers. We can help them understand us: who we are (now), who we were (when we were younger), what we like and dislike, what our hopes and desires for the future are, and how we want to have a say in how we are cared for down the road. If you take time now — before anything happens to drastically change your life (or changes it further) — it is possible that you can provide critically important information and data that future caregivers can put to use in order to provide a more positive and rewarding experience for you. You can have influence on your future caregiving. What a fantastic concept.

Who Cares: A Loving Guide for My Future Caregivers was created by Dee Marrella after having gone through the caregiving process. The experience left her with many wonderful memories, but also left her with a number of unanswered questions and a burning need to help others address the needs those being cared for have. This book — this guide — reflects Dee's experiences and the influence others with whom Dee has met with and heard from. This is a tool. And like any tool, it can't do it's intended job if it isn't put to work.

If you are the individual filling out the pages of this guide, I am sure that your future caregivers will appreciate your efforts. If you have acquired this book for someone else, rest assured that you are giving them something that they and their caregivers will find extremely valuable. (However, if you are only giving this to someone else, I strongly urge you to fill one out for yourself. If you intend to help another person…why not help yourself as well?)

In the first edition, I reprinted an article that Dee had read in *The Philadelphia Inquirer*. The author of the article, Dan Gottlieb, a clinical psychologist from Philadelphia, gave us permission to reprint his thoughts. The article is entitled:

A father, a son, and a vacation that won't be forgotten

Vacation is over and I am a little sad. That's not news. Everyone is a little sad after vacation. I am not sad about returning to work, I am sad about leaving my vacation roommate. For the past month, I have been living with my 88-year-old father.

Several years ago I never would have believed such a time could be filled with joy. That's because when my mother died in January 1998, my father was consumed with grief. After 56 years of being in a loving marriage, it was almost a year before he could hear her name without crying. His grief was raw and deep. But something good came out of the process. He and I were always close, but after her death we became even closer. For the first time in our relationship, he would share his sadness, regret and fear of the future.

As his grief diminished, he met a "friend," whom he would occasionally take to dinner. His friend became much more than that, and, in our daily phone conversations, he would excitedly talk about his new relationship and his redis-covered libido! For the first time in years, he was animated and happy. One day about a year ago, while we were driv-ing together, he got frustrated and said: "I don't even know why I am pursuing this relationship. I can't have sex any-way." I thought that, after 55 years, it was time to have "the talk." It was both awkward and tender as a paralyzed son talked to a father who'd had his prostate removed about what it really means to have sex. We talked about some of the many ways people find pleasure and love each other.

Despite his joy, I had watched with sadness and con-cern as his 88 years began to take their toll on his body. Although his mind remained clear, his vision and hearing both diminished and he developed a heart condition. Maybe that's what got me thinking about my dream.

Ever since I graduated from Atlantic City High School in 1964, I have dreamed about returning to the Shore for the summer. Despite my father's advancing age, I probably would have postponed my dream a few more years. But several months ago I learned that a friend of mine had died. This was a fellow quadriplegic — a man my age who had gone through rehabilitation with me. When his daughter informed me of his death, she said: "After 20 years as a quadriplegic, his body just gave out." I have been a quadriplegic for 22 years.

Later that day, I remembered a bumper sticker someone sent me years ago: "Don't postpone joy." So I called my father, who still lives in Atlantic City, and asked him how he felt about making his apartment wheelchair-accessible and spending the month of July with me. He was thrilled.

As the time drew closer, he grew more excited and I grew more concerned. He told me he was intending to cancel all his plans for the month so we could be together. I told him that although I wanted to spend time with him, I also needed time alone. I worried that his lifestyle had become restricted and the month would be depressing.

In the beginning of July, I arrived to discover that my concerns about his being intrusive on my time were unfounded. His relationship with his friend didn't last very long, but his libido sure did! Now he has other "friends." I watched with delight as he went out for various meals and activities with different friends while I stayed home or went to the movies.

Over the course of the month we became roommates in every sense of the word. I teased him about his memory and he teased me when I left the screen door open and I hollered at him for being too rigid about time. We shared jokes, lunches, and we worried about each other.

But mostly we just talked. At the time, it seemed like what we talked about was not very important — where he was going to dinner, what television shows he liked, how he dealt with his insomnia, and various other chronic problems. But as I look back on those talks I realize that he was telling me about his life — the same way I told him about my life when I was in college.

Now I know that he religiously watches Jeopardy! When he is not out on a date. And that his brother calls at exactly 9 every morning. I know that he loves to read murder mysteries and always reads the last page first to make sure it has a happy ending. Little bits of information that seem trivial. As I leave the apartment, I have a picture of a day in his life. I also have other pictures etched in my memory from this vacation. I watched as he sat in his lounge chair holding his book 12 inches from his face, moving his head from side to side, drinking in each line. I watched as he slept in that same chair with the book in his lap. I watched as he sometimes stared out the window, lost in his own thoughts, his face reflecting whether he was thinking about his past or his future.

And I watched the animation as he spoke on the phone to one of his friends, and his loud laughter when he heard something funny or ribald. Each one of these observations felt like a snapshot in my mind that I pray will not fade when his chair is empty.

Best vacation I ever had.

Thanks, Dad.

Reading Dan's article immediately created mental flashbacks — to my mother's lengthy illness, her demanding caregiving needs, and slow, painful death. It made me recall my father's outpatient surgery that went seriously wrong and the challenge the family faced with intensive care demands and his unexpected death. Suddenly the purpose of Dee Marrella's guidebook became crystal clear. All the memories, the great stories, the mental images — that's all that we had left. What about the basic facts of their lives — some that we couldn't recall? If only some of them had been written down.

This is one of the reasons that this guide is so very important. It provides a stimulus that we all need to set down in writing — the thoughts and memories, the needs and desires that our future caregivers will use to serve us better. This is a golden opportunity to actually speak into the future — when, perhaps we cannot speak for ourselves.

It is my sincere hope that each person who picks up a copy of **Who Cares** will be inspired to put down in writing those seemingly-insignificant or trivial facts and bits of data about themselves so that one day those words might make all the difference in the world to a caregiver who reads them — and to YOU.

— **Dennis N. McClellan**
Publisher

A PERSONAL NOTE TO MY FUTURE CAREGIVERS

*W*hen I am in need of your care, I realize there will be times when I exasperate you, and you get annoyed with my table manners, forgetfulness, etc. When this happens, would you take a few minutes to read the following poem? An elderly woman in a nursing home wrote it. When she passed away, the poem was found tucked inside her Bible. Perhaps reading this poem every so often will help you rekindle your feelings of understanding and sympathy. Your responsibilities while caring for me will sometimes seem overwhelming. Any "tool" I can give to you to help you function makes me feel better.

Signature _____

SOMETHING TO THINK ABOUT

What Do You See Nurse?

What do you see nurse, what do you see?

What are you thinking when you look at me?

A crabby old woman, not very wise,

uncertain of habit, with far away eyes,

who dribbles her food, and makes no reply,

when you say in a loud voice, "I do wish you'd try!!"

Who seems not to notice the things that you do,

and forever is losing a stocking or shoe.

Who, unresisting or not, lets you do as you will

with bathing and feeding, the long day to fill.

Is that what you're thinking, is that what you see?

WHO CARES

Then open your eyes, you're not looking at me.

I'll tell you who I am as I sit here so still,

as I move at your bidding, as I eat at your will.

I am a small child of ten with a father and mother,

brothers and sisters who love one another.

A young girl of sixteen with wings on her feet,

dreaming that soon now a lover she'll meet.

A bride soon at twenty, my heart gives a leap,

remembering the vows that I promised to keep.

At twenty-five now I have young of my own,

who need me to build a secure, happy home.

A woman of thirty, my young now grow fast,

bound to each other with ties that should last.

At forty now my young soon will be gone,

but my man stays beside me to see I don't mourn.

At fifty once more babies play round my knee,

again we know children, my loved one and me.

Dark days are upon me, my husband is dead,

I look at my future, I shudder with dread.

For my young are all busy rearing young of their own,

and I think of the years and the love I have known.

I'm an old lay now and nature is cruel,

"Tis her jest to make old age look like a fool."

The body it crumbles, grace and vigor depart,

and now there is stone where I once had a heart.

But inside this old body a young girl still dwells,

and now and again my battered heart swells.

I remember the joys, I remember the pain,

and I am loving and living life over again.

I think of the years all too few, gone so fast,

and I am loving and living life over again.

I think of the years all too few, gone so fast,

and accept the stark fact that nothing can last.

So open you eyes nurse, open and see,

not a crabby old woman, look closer, see Me.

— **Anonymous**

PART I
General Instructions

Sometimes life has a way of putting us on our backs in order to force us to look up.

Charles L. Allen

SUGGESTIONS

1. Complete this book **NOW** — not later.

2. Place this guide where future caregivers can easily find it.

3. Update the contents once a year, if possible. (Very few things will change.)

4. Remember to tell your caregivers that they are all just human beings. If they have done all they can to love you, comfort you, and help you maintain your *dignity* — ***they can not do more***.

5. If you are a parent raising a child with mental or any other serious medical challenge, you are always very concerned (Who will take care of my child if I become seriously ill or die first?) Fill out a copy of this book for that child, in addition to completing one for yourself. You will not regret this future caregivers will be grateful fo the information provided by a loving parent about the habits, needs, and interests of the child.

A LETTER TO MY FUTURE CAREGIVERS

*T*HE FOLLOWING LETTER WAS written to my three daughters, Tammy, Lani and Robin. I wrote it with love from the bottom of my heart. It will go inside my personal copy of **Who Cares**.

Write a similar letter now, while you are able to convey your true feelings. Do not worry about spelling or grammar. Just say what is in your heart. It will mean so much later on. Just do it!

The letter begins on the following page …

Dear Tammy, Lani and Robin,

One of my deepest fears is the thought of one day growing old and helpless. I pray that God takes me first. However, there is a strong possibility that He will not. In that case, I want to make the burden of your caring for me as easy and gentle as possible.

When Grandmom became "dead weight" and she had to enter a nursing home, I think you can remember how much it broke my heart. She always asked my sisters and me to promise never to put her into a nursing home. I promised, with sincere, loving intentions — but could not keep *my promise when she was beyond my physical and mental capabilities. I never want any of you to proclaim that you would never put your mother or father in a nursing home. Sometimes it will be beyond your control. All I ask is that you research and find a home that "feels right" for me. Is the staff friendly? Do the residents look clean and content? Are there visitors around? If possible, I would like a private room. (You know how I react to bad odors, etc.) Please keep air fresheners and potpourri in my room.*

When you come to visit, please don't tell me you can't stay very long. That tells me that you are there because of obligation. Truthfully, in that case, I would rather you stay away and get whatever is rushing you out of the way. Just come and see me when you can spend quality time holding my hand, talking to me and seeing that I am okay. I say all of the above with love and understanding — not with anger.

Remember that your husband and children take priority. I know what it was like juggling children's activities, meals, household necessities, husband's needs, and to worry and feel guilty about my sick mother. Remember when Grandmom Bea was in the nursing home? I was living in Pennsylvania. Your Dad and I decided that I would leave Pennsylvania every Monday morning and spend Monday and Tuesday in New Jersey with Grandmom. I would pick her up at 9:30 AM and take her back at 4 PM. Each day I would try to plan to have some of her *friends meet us at the mall. This sometimes became difficult because she was 91 and most of her friends had passed away. Anyway, by Tuesday at 4 PM, when I dropped her off before heading back to PA, I was exhausted and filled with guilt about having to leave her. I never left her once when she said, "Thank you for coming. I had a nice time. I'll see you next time." She would always look depressed and would say, "Why do you always have to leave so soon?" I realized she didn't want to be where she was. She was always such an alive, active person. I would drive home crying and feeling guilty. I never want you girls to feel that way. I thank you, from the bottom of my heart, for **any quality time*** you will give me in the future. Never feel guilty when you have to leave.

If I am visiting in your home, please talk to me. I may get deaf and I might have weak eyesight, but I can cope with these. I could not cope, however, with being tolerated or forgotten. I desire to be a viable member of the family. I want my grandchildren to love me and want to be around me. Laughter is such a healer. It bothers me so much to see older people sitting amongst others and just listening and not joining in. (Do they feel left out? Do they not want to interact? What makes them feel this way?)

Tammy, Lani and Robin — I want to thank you for being such wonderful daughters. You *have always been there when Dad and I needed you. When you heard about Dad's heart operation, Tammy, you organized a schedule so that each of you would spend one week with me. By the end of three weeks, Dad was well on his way to recovery. Lani and Robin — remember when you got the initial call saying Dad had his heart attack? You came right to the hospital in Pennsylvania from New Jersey without packing or grabbing your purses. That shows how little you thought of yourselves at a time when you were needed.*

Very often a little old lady sat in a wheelchair by the main entry to Grandmom's nursing home. I would give her a big greeting and hug each time I saw her. One day she

•9•

grabbed my arm and pulled me back. She said, "I want you to promise to remember what I am going to tell you. When they put me in this nursing home, they took away my house, my car, my furniture — but they couldn't take away my memories. Go out and get as many good memories as you can."

Tammy, Lani and Robin — thank you for being such loving daughters. I have many wonderful, happy memories of times shared with you. I love you!

Mom

PS: Always help each other.

PERSONAL LETTER TO MY FUTURE CAREGIVERS

Date: _____

Dear: _____

_____

_____

_____

_____

_____

_____

_____

WHO CARES

GENERAL INSTRUCTIONS

WHO CARES

FOR MY CAREGIVERS: WHAT I HAVE LEARNED IN LIFE

*T*HE FOLLOWING LIST is offered as an example of my own personal beliefs! You should feel free to express your own outlook on life to your future caregivers on the pages that follow.

- Teach your children that respect and manners do not cost a dime — but oh how far they will take them in life.

- In large decisions in life, decide what is in your heart. Do not just think with your head.

- No one can take the place of a Mom or Dad in raising children.

- Do not do anything you would not be proud to have your children do in the future. They are watching.

- Raise your children to be proud of his/her faith, religion and nationality. Be an example.

- A child is blessed if he/she is intelligent. If this child, however, is self-centered, selfish or disrespectful, he or she will be viewed as a failure.

- Do not rush through life. Enjoy each other. Enjoy your children. Make "happy memories" together. Laugh and cry together. Cherish the time you have together. It goes by so quickly.

- Instill in each other that, between family members, there should never be "measuring." Never measure: who called last; who entertained last, who got what. Be there to help in time of need. Be there to share when you can give your time. Be a "cheerleader" for each other.

GENERAL INSTRUCTIONS

- Expect respect from your children. They will thank you later.

- Do not have children you do not have time for. Raising a child properly is the hardest, but most gratifying, job in the whole world.

- Try not to build walls between your children and you. Listen when they want to talk to you. Do not slough off something that is bothering them as silly. Show them the respect and understanding they need.

- Teach your children to view all humans as equals. We are all here to live a life to its fullest. Teach them to despise hateful behavior. Teach them respect for race and religion. There is so much to gain if we all learn from and respect each other.

WHO CARES

WHAT I HAVE
LEARNED IN LIFE
MY PERSONAL BELIEFS:

_____

_____

_____

_____

_____

_____

_____

_____

_____

_____

PRIORITIES FOR CARE

WHO CARES

PART II
Priorities for Care

*Those who bring sunshine to the lives of others
cannot keep it from themselves.*

James M. Barrie

Address each section below as completely as
possible

Note: Update this section whenever there is a change in
medication, attending physicians, etc.

> ☛ Making medical decisions for an incompetent
> loved one can be an anguishing task for a caretaker.

Physical problems I have and medications I take for them (include all prescription and across-the-counter drugs):

Allergies I have and medications I take for them (include all prescription and across-the-counter drugs):

My family history of reproductive problems (miscarriages, stillbirths, infertility, birth defects):

My family history of diseases (diabetes, cardiac, mental challenges, etc.):

MY FAVORITE
PRODUCT BRANDS

Toothpaste: _____

Mouthwash: _____

Laxative: _____

Headache Remedy: _____

Vitamins:
      General Multivitamin: _____
      Vitamin C: _____
      Other: _____
      Other: _____
      Other: _____

Deodorant: _____

Perfume/Cologne/Aftershave Lotion: _____

Lipstick Color: _____

PRIORITIES FOR CARE

Makeup:

     1. _____

     2. _____

     3. _____

Hair Coloring Kit: _____

Hairspray: _____

Nail Polish: _____

Moisturizer: _____

Razor: _____

Shaving Cream: _____

Facial Hair Remover: _____

Soap: _____

Other Items: _____

_____

IF I HAD
A TERMINAL ILLNESS

_____ I would want to know.

_____ I would not want to know.

Comments on above:

_____

_____

_____

_____

_____

_____

_____

Would I want you to request any hospital or doctor to keep me alive through extreme means if I were suffering?

_____ Yes _____ No

Comments on use of life support:

_____

_____

_____

_____

_____

_____

_____

_____

_____

PRIORITY FOR CARE

WHAT IS A "LIVING WILL?"

A "LIVING WILL" IS A DOCUMENT (*also known as an advanced directive*) *that states in advance of a serious illness or accident what medical treatments you want or don't want to receive. It can also be a document in which the signer requests to be allowed to die rather than be kept alive by artificial means if disabled beyond a reasonable expectation of recovery. When signed by a competent person, it can provide guidance for medical and health-care decisions (as the termination of life support or organ donation) in the event the person becomes incompetent to make such decisions.*

A simple statement could be created and signed in front of witnesses. It is recommended that two witnesses also sign the document. Those witnesses should not be direct members of your family or someone who would benefit financially in the event of your death.

NOTE: *It is very important to understand that if you fail to make a living will accessible to others, it is actually of no value and becomes completely worthless. Copies of your living will should be (1) kept with this guide and (2) given to any member of your immediate family that you feel should have one, (3) to your primary care physician and any specialists you work with, (4) your attorney, (5) and the hospital to which you feel you would most likely be taken in case of an emergency. If you are admitted to a nursing home, make sure the administration has a copy. It wouldn't be a bad idea to carry a copy in your purse or wallet.*

Always discuss any matters of a legal nature with an attorney of your choice.

☛ Many people today are worried about the medical care they would be given if they should become terminally ill and unable to communicate. They don't want to spend months or years dependent on life-supporting machines, and they don't want to cause unnecessary emotional or financial stress for their loved ones.

—American Hospital Association
"Put It in Writing: Questions and Answers or Advance Directives"

"Do I want my doctors to keep me alive through artificial means if I become seriously ill or injured?"

_____ Yes   _____ No

Specifically, I want the following to be done:

- If my heart stops, I do _____ do not _____ want CPR (cardio-pulmonary resuscitation).

- I do _____ do not _____ want to be placed on any mechanical breathing apparatus.

- I do _____ do not _____ wish to have any blood transfusions.

- I do _____ do not _____ want any intravenous food administered.

- I do _____ do not _____ want any liquids administered intravenously.

- If I am transported to a healthcare facility and placed on life support, I do _____ do not _____ want it stopped at the directive of my representative(s).

Comments on this subject:

I Would Like to Be an Organ Donor.

_____ Yes   _____ No

Comments on Organ Donation:

Any Special Requests Regarding Organ Donation:

MY PREFERRED HEALTHCARE PROVIDERS

Physician: Name_____
Phone_____
Address_____
_____

Dentist: Name_____
Phone_____
Address_____
_____

Podiatrist: Name_____
Phone_____
Address_____
_____

PRIORITIES FOR CARE

Optometrist: Name _____
Phone _____
Address _____

_____

Optician: Name _____
Phone _____
Address _____

_____

Pharmacy: Name _____
Phone _____
Address _____

_____

Hospital: Name _____
Phone _____
Address _____

_____

Other: Name _____
Phone _____
Address _____

_____

DOCTORS, HOSPITALS, OTHER PROFESSIONALS THAT I **NEVER** WANT TO GO BACK TO:

Name_____
Phone_____
Address_____
_____

Name_____
Phone_____
Address_____
_____

Name_____
Phone_____
Address_____
_____

MY THOUGHTS ON A NURSING HOME OR ALTERNATIVE LIVING FACILITY AND MY PERSONAL CARE PRIORITIES:

PRIORITY FOR CARE

WHO CARES

PART III
My Preferences

Always be a little kinder than necessary.

James M. Barrie

IMPORTANT HOUSEHOLD INFORMATION:

Garage Door Opener Combination: _____

_____

Location of Fusebox: _____

_____

Location of Water Shut-off: _____

Plumber: Name _____
              Phone _____

Electrician: Name _____
              Phone _____

Maintenance Person:
              Name _____
              Phone _____

Heating and Air Conditioning Company:

Name _____

Phone _____

Electric Company:

Name _____

Phone _____

Gas Company:

Name _____

Phone _____

Lawn Care Company:

Name _____

Phone _____

Additional Information: _____

_____

_____

_____

MY PREFERENCES

EXAMPLES OF FOOD
I ENJOY:

For Breakfast:

For Lunch:

For Dinner:

Foods I love and would eat at any time:

Foods I *absolutely hate* and would never eat:

Foods I am allergic to:

My favorite snack foods include:

My favorite soups are:

My favorite salads and dressings include:

My favorite entrees are:

My favorite:

    Candy:

    Cake:

Pie: ✍ _____

_____

Ice Cream: ✍ _____

_____

When you have me in your home, here are some recipes that I really enjoy: (Write in complete recipes that you've created or make regularly, or make reference to recipes that are familiar to family members. Attach a memory that went along with each recipe.)

Note: Don't hesitate to use additional sheets of paper if needed to complete your recipes.

✍ _____

_____

_____

_____

_____

_____

_____

WHO CARES

MY PREFERENCES

WHO CARES

_____

_____

_____

_____

_____

_____

_____

_____

_____

_____

_____

_____

_____

_____

_____

MY CLOTHING SIZES

Female

_____ Dress
_____ Blouse
_____ Slacks
_____ Outer Coat
_____ Sweater
_____ Shoes
_____ Stockings
_____ Pajamas
_____ Nightgown
_____ Slippers
_____ Housecoat
_____ Slips
_____ Underpants
_____ Bras

Male

_____ Suit
_____ Shirt
_____ Trousers
_____ Outer Coat
_____ Sweater
_____ Shoes
_____ Socks
_____ Pajamas

_____ Slippers
_____ Robe
_____ Underwear
_____ T-Shirts
Shorts
_____ Boxer
_____ Briefs

MY PREFERENCES

• 51 •

WHERE TO FIND THINGS IN MY HOUSE/APARTMENT:

Medication(s)

Extra eye glasses:

Dentures:

Hearing Aid:

Walker:

Folding Wheelchair:

Insulin Equipment:

Other:

Bedtime clothing I feel most comfortable wearing (Put in order of favorites — "1" being your favorite):

_____ Nightgown
_____ Pajamas
_____ Underwear
_____ Other

My Favorite Bed Pillow: (Check one)

_____ Soft
_____ Medium
_____ Hard

I like to take: (Check one)

_____ Showers
_____ Baths

Comments on Above:

_____

_____

_____

Clothes I am most comfortable in:

Clothes I *do not* like to wear:

MY PREFERENCES

My favorite colors to wear:

Three favorite outfits I like to wear:

1.

2.

3.

In a nursing home, you are given one small closet (as a rule) and one dresser. What would you choose to put in these places if you had to sort through all your clothes, jewelry, books, etc. today?

What would you want on the walls of your room? (Include favorite family picture, a favorite clock, etc.) Where are these items found in your current home or apartment?

Are there any religious items that you want to always have near you? Please list and identify where they can be located.

Ways I like to relax:

Types of TV shows I enjoy:

_____

_____

_____

_____

_____

_____

Favorite movies and videos I enjoy viewing:

_____

_____

_____

_____

_____

_____

_____

Favorite TV channels and shows:

_____

_____

_____

_____

_____

_____

Sports I like to watch (on TV or in person):

Sport   **Favorite Team**

_____

_____

_____

_____

_____

_____

Favorite TV stars:

Favorite movie stars:

Types of TV shows / Movies that I *do not* enjoy:

Radio programs I enjoy:

Radio programs I *do not* enjoy:

Music I enjoy listening to:

Music that gives me a headache:

Favorite singers:

_____

_____

_____

_____

_____

_____

Newspapers and Magazines I enjoy reading:

_____

_____

_____

_____

_____

_____

My favorite authors:

My favorite religious passages, scriptures, meditations, readings:

Card games I enjoy:

_____

_____

_____

_____

_____

Board games I enjoy:

_____

_____

_____

_____

_____

Do you like to be around small children?

Do you like to be around animals?

	Yes	No
Dogs		
Cats		
Other		

CARING FOR MY PETS
IN A TIME OF EMERGENCY

Type of pet: _____

Name of pet: _____

Veterinarian: Name _____

Phone _____

Address _____

_____

Pet Groomer: Name _____

Phone _____

Address _____

_____

Kennel: Name _____

Phone _____

Address _____

_____

Name and telephone number of individual who *could* care for pet temporarily:

Name _____

Phone _____

Address _____

_____

Brand of General Pet Food:

Dry _____

_____

Wet _____

_____

Brand of Biscuits: _____

Brand of Special Treats: _____

Exercise habits: _____

_____

_____

Where he/she prefers to sleep: _____

_____

_____

Would you like your pet to visit you if possible?

_____ Yes _____ No

Arrangements for permanent care for my pet — to assure that my pet is loved and properly cared for:

_____

_____

_____

_____

_____

_____

_____

_____

_____

_____

_____

PLACES I LIKE TO VISIT

Where I like to go for drives in the car:

For breakfast (name restaurants):

For lunch (name restaurants):

For dinner (name restaurants):

_____

_____

_____

For sightseeing:

_____

_____

_____

FUNERAL ARRANGEMENTS THAT I PREFER

I would like to be:

_____ **Buried**
Location _____
City / State _____

_____ **Cremated**
Location _____
City / State _____

Note: if any prior arrangements have been made, where can those documents be located, including plans for ashes if cremated:

_____

_____

_____

I would like to wear the color(s):

_____

_____

_____

I would like this church/temple/place of worship to be used for the ceremony (name of location, city):

Location _____

City / State _____

_____

I would like this Priest, Rabbi, Clergyman to preside over the ceremony:

Name _____

Phone _____

Address _____

_____

I would like the following Funeral Home and Funeral Director:

Name

Phone

Address

I would like the following flowers:

I would like the following music played at the place of worship:

I would like these prayers said at my funeral:

I would like to have the following inscribed on my tombstone or grave marker:

_____

_____

_____

_____

I would like the following donations made in my memory (list organizations, groups, individuals):

_____

_____

_____

_____

_____

_____

I want these items placed in the coffin with me:

_____

_____

_____

I would prefer "at the viewing":

_____An open casket   _____ A closed casket

_____I prefer no viewing

_____I pefer a memorial service rather than a viewing

   _____ Casket or cremation vessel present

   _____ No Casket or cremation vessel present

My children are buried (location, city):

      Location _____

      City / State _____

My parents are buried (location, city):

      Location _____

      City / State _____

PART IV
Who Am I?

The only gift is a portion of thyself.

Ralph Waldo Emerson

WHO AM I?
MY TYPICAL DAY

I think it important for any caregiver to understand what my typical day is like and how much it means that these routine activities and rituals be maintained as much as possible.

- I usually wake at _____ AM.

- I like eating breakfast at _____ AM.

- Most mornings I enjoy: (examples: gardening, watching TV, reading newspapers)

  _____

  _____

  _____

- I like to eat my lunch at _____ AM or PM.

WHO AM I?

🐝 I enjoy an afternoon nap at _____ PM.

🐝 Most afternoons I enjoy:

_____

_____

_____

🐝 I like to eat dinner at _____ PM.

🐝 After dinner I enjoy:

_____

_____

_____

🐝 I usually get ready for bed at _____ PM.

🐝 I like to:

Read in bed _____ (yes or no)

Watch TV in bed _____ (yes or no)

Go right to sleep _____ (yes or no)

WHO AM I?

I speak on the phone daily to the following people:

Name _____

Relationship _____

Phone # _____

Name _____

Relationship _____

Phone # _____

Name _____

Relationship _____

Phone # _____

WHO AM I?
MY TALENTS AND INTERESTS

Musical Instruments I play (or played):

_____

_____

_____

_____

Singing Ability:

_____

_____

_____

_____

_____

WHO AM I?

Acting Ability:

_____

_____

_____

_____

Other Talents/Skills:

_____

_____

_____

_____

Hobbies:

_____

_____

_____

_____

WHO AM I?

MILTARY HISTORY(if applicable)

I served in the:

_____ Army

_____ Navy

_____ Marines

_____ Merchant Marines

_____ Coast Guard

_____ Other Service _____

My rank at discharge was:

_____

My discharge date was (day, month, year):

_____

My discharge papers are filed (location):

_____

I belong to the following veterans'
organizations:

_____

_____

_____

I am receiving the following pension or
military disability benefits:

_____

_____

Any survivor benefits (list if "yes"):

_____

_____

_____

WHO AM I?

What are my innermost feelings about myself? What are the things about myself that I like and dislike? And what do I like and dislike about the world around me?

Keep in mind that you will have your own feelings to write down. It is also important to note that there is no set number of responses, and no response is "right" or "wrong." The following are the authors examples:

🥀 *I am very "thin skinned." My feelings can get hurt very easily. Because I am this way, I try to "feel" for others and not offend them.*

🥀 *I believe every child should get a fine education. Equally important, however, I believe every child should be taught the importance of manners and honesty — or you, as a parent, have "shortchanged" your child.*

🐚 *God gave each of us special talents. It is a sin if you do not use these talents to make the world a better place.*

🐚 *One of the most evil things on this earth is prejudice. I try to look each person squarely in the eye and decide if I like or dislike what I see. I think it is so wrong to judge a person because of his/her color, religion or nationality. We could learn so much from each other.*

🐚 *I am afraid of animals. I love to watch them. I would never harm them. I was never allowed to have a pet as a child. Therefore, I keep my distance.*

WHO AM I?

Here are my innermost likes and dislikes about myself and the world around me.

WHO CARES

FEARS I HAVE

Keep in mind that you will have your own fears to share. It is also important to note that there is no set number of fears, and no response is "right" or "wrong." The following are the author's examples.

- *I am not afraid of death. I am afraid of pain and suffering. Medicate me, even if it means a shorter life*

- *Being treated like a child in my later life is a fear I have. Please never talk down to me or "pat me on the head." Allow me to keep my dignity.*

- *Make certain that I am never fed anything with a Red Sauce or Mayonnaise. I gag on both.*

WHO AM I?

I *am very shy. If possible, please do not let a male nurse care for me.*

I *fear strife in the family if Dad or I were alone and sickly. Our family has such love and closeness now. Please do not let Dad or me cause that to change. Work together. Try to keep a sense of humor. Two things have always helped me when things got really stressful with Gram: faith in God and a good laugh.*

FEARS I HAVE

WHO CARES

ONE SPECIFIC FEAR

One of the greatest fears people have for the future is being told that you have Alzheimer's. How can one prepare for this? How can you help your "caregivers?"

I spoke with an individual who works with Alzheimer's patients. She said that one could never predict when the patient is lucid or when the person is living in his/her past. Claudia recommended that I include this section in this guide so that the caregiver can talk and reminisce about the past with the patient. She said it would be very helpful to have an idea of what the person was like in his/her teens, 20's, 30's, etc.

Here are things I want you to know about me when I was:

IN MY TEENS:

I lived in:

City / State _____

High School and year of graduation:

Name / Date _____

My favorite date was (his/her name):

_____

My favorite thing to do on a date was:

_____

For fun, my friends and I would:

_____

My interests and hobbies were:

_____

Additional information:

_____

_____

_____

_____

WHO AM I?

IN MY 20's:

I lived in:

 City / State _____

I worked at:

 Company/Job _____

I married: _____

on _____. (month/day/year)

My children's names are:

 _____ /DOB _____

 _____ /DOB _____

 _____ /DOB _____

 _____ /DOB _____

My friends included:

 _____

 _____

 _____

 _____

For fun, my friends and I would:

My interests and hobbies were:

Additional information:

IN MY 30's:

I lived in:

City / State _____

I worked at:

Company/Job _____

I married: _____

on _____. (month/day/year)

My children's names are:

_____ /DOB _____

_____ /DOB _____

_____ /DOB _____

_____ /DOB _____

My friends included:

_____

_____

_____

_____

WHO AM I?

For fun, my friends and I would:

My interests and hobbies were:

Additional information:

IN MY 40's:

I lived in:

City / State _____

I worked at:

Company/Job _____

My grandchildren's names are:

_____ /DOB _____

_____ /DOB _____

_____ /DOB _____

_____ /DOB _____

My friends included:

_____

_____

_____

_____

WHO AM I?

For fun, my friends and I would:

My interests and hobbies were:

Additional information:

IN MY 50's:

I lived in:

🐌   City / State _____

I worked at:

🐌   Company/Job _____

My grandchildren's names are:

🐌   _____ /DOB _____

🐌   _____ /DOB _____

🐌   _____ /DOB _____

🐌   _____ /DOB _____

My friends included:

🐌   _____

🐌   _____

🐌   _____

🐌   _____

WHO AM I?

For fun, my friends and I would:

_____

_____

_____

_____

_____

_____

My interests and hobbies were:

_____

_____

_____

_____

Additional information:

_____

_____

_____

_____

_____

IN MY 60's:

I lived in:

City / State _____

I worked at:

Company/Job _____

My grandchildren's names are:

_____ /DOB _____

_____ /DOB _____

_____ /DOB _____

_____ /DOB _____

My friends included:

_____

_____

_____

_____

WHO AM I?

For fun, my friends and I would:

_____

_____

_____

_____

_____

_____

My interests and hobbies were:

_____

_____

_____

_____

Additional information:

_____

_____

_____

_____

_____

IN MY 70's:

I lived in:

City / State _____

I worked at:

Company/Job _____

My grandchildren's names (Great grandchildren if there are any) are:

_____ /DOB _____

_____ /DOB _____

_____ /DOB _____

_____ /DOB _____

My friends included:

_____

_____

_____

_____

For fun, my friends and I would:

_____

_____

_____

_____

_____

_____

My interests and hobbies were:

_____

_____

_____

_____

Additional information:

_____

_____

_____

_____

_____

IN MY 80's:

I lived in:

🐾 City / State _____

My grandchildren's names (Great grandchildren if there are any) are:

🐾 _____ /DOB _____

🐾 _____ /DOB _____

🐾 _____ /DOB _____

🐾 _____ /DOB _____

My friends included:

🐾 _____

🐾 _____

🐾 _____

🐾 _____

WHO AM I?

For fun, my friends and I would:

My interests and hobbies were:

Additional information:

SPECIAL REQUESTS FOR CAREGIVERS

Keep in mind that those special requests you have for your own family will be different than these. You may have more; you may have less. It's quality, not quantity that counts here.

I have always taught my daughters that you will never, ever find more reliable sincere friends than your own sisters or brothers. My request: "Please do not ever close the lines of communications with one another. If something is bothering you, talk it out — together."

Never measure what you do for each other. Give with your whole heart when a family member is in need.

- I *would enjoy receiving* Holy Communion *when it is offered*.

- *Always make faith and religion a* **family priority**.

SPECIAL REQUESTS
FOR CAREGIVERS

WHO CARES

PART V
Relationships

Whatever you do to the least of my brothers...
that you do unto me.

Jesus

IMPORTANT QUESTION: IF YOU ARE ILL OR GETTING OLDER

1. Would you want to stay in familiar surroundings, but living far away from loved ones, or

2. Move close to family

Explain:

PEOPLE I LOVE AND WOULD ENJOY SEEING:

Name_____

Phone_____

Address_____

_____

Name_____

Phone_____

Address_____

_____

Name_____

Phone_____

Address_____

_____

Name_____

Phone_____

Address_____

_____

RELATIONSHIPS

FRIENDS TO NOTIFY
IF I AM HOSPITALIZED:

Name_____

Phone_____

Address_____

_____

Name_____

Phone_____

Address_____

_____

Name_____

Phone_____

Address_____

_____

Name_____

Phone_____

Address_____

_____

IF ANYONE INVITED ME TO GO OUT FOR A DAY'S OUTING OR EVENING, THIS IS WHAT I WOULD REALLY ENJOY DOING:

In town:

On a trip:

PART VI
Holidays and
Religious Observances

My favorite holiday:

_____

_____

_____

_____

_____

_____

_____

Why this holiday has always been so special:

_____

_____

_____

_____

_____

_____

_____

What I love to do on my favorite holiday:

TRADITIONAL FAMILY HOLIDAYS

NOTE: For many people, Thanksgiving and Halloween are holidays that are observed. However, since there are many holidays throughout any given year, and considering that we all celebrate different ones in our own family structure, please fill in the ones you are most familiar with below.

Holiday_____

Family Tradition Observed_____

_____

_____

_____

_____

_____

HOLIDAYS AND RELIGIOUS OBSERVANCES

Holiday

Family Tradition Observed

Holiday

Family Tradition Observed

Holiday_____

Family Tradition Observed_____

_____

_____

_____

_____

_____

_____

Holiday_____

Family Tradition Observed:_____

_____

_____

_____

_____

_____

_____

RELIGIOUS AFFILIATION

Church/Temple/Religious Facility:

Address: _____

Telephone #: _____

e-mail: _____

Key Contact Names: _____

_____

_____

Describe Attendance (include time of day, seating area, and other important points):

_____

_____

_____

_____

Describe Participation (such as choir, usher, etc.):

Interesting and memorable times I would love to talk about with anyone who would listen:

_____

_____

_____

_____

_____

_____

I once read somewhere that the nicest things you could give an elderly loved one include:

- Your time

- Hugs and hand holding

- Time to talk, listen and reminisce about the past and happy times

Holiday vacation I enjoy the most (such as a visit to the seashore, a visit to the mountains, taking a cruise. etc.):

PART VII
Important Names

CHART OF DECENDANTS (**SAMPLE** FAMILY TREE)

Elvira Amendola		Daymond Delia
Mother		*Father*

Their Children

Theresa Delia	Delores Delia(me)	Karen Delia
	married	
	Leonard S. Marrella	

My Children

Tammy Marrella	Lani Marrella	Robin Marrella
Toso	Martin	Russo

My Grandchildren

Tory Toso	Len Belotti	Ryan Russo
Todd Toso	Roseanne Martin	Casey Russo
	Danielle Martin	

My Birth:
St. Joseph's Hosital
Paterson, New Jersey
December 4th, 1935

YOUR CHART OF DECENDANTS

Mother   Father

Their Children

(me)

married

My Children

My Grandchildren

My Birth:

PERSONAL INFORMATION

Last Name: _____

First Name: _____

Middle Name: _____

Nickname: _____

Named After: _____

Birth Date: _____

Current Address: _____

_____

_____

Current Telephone Number: _____

E-mail Address: _____

Location of Birth Certificate: _____

Profession: _____

Marriage

Location: _____

Date: _____

Location of Marriage Certificate: _____

_____

Previous Spouse (If Applicable):

Name: _____

Address: _____

SPOUSE'S INFORMATION

Last Name: _____

First Name: _____

Middle Name: _____

Nickname: _____

Named After: _____

Birth Date: _____

Current Address: _____

_____

Current Telephone Number: _____
Profession: _____

E-mail Address: _____

EDUCATION

Elementary School

Name: _____

Location: _____

Junior High or Middle School

Name: _____

Location: _____

High School

Name: _____

Location: _____

College/University

Undergraduate:

      Location: _____

      Major: _____

      Minor: _____

      Degree Received: _____

      Honors: _____

Graduate:

      Location: _____

      Major: _____

      Minor: _____

      Degree Received: _____

CAREER — JOBS HELD

Company Name:

    Location: _____

    Job Title/Description: _____

    Years Employed There: _____

Company Name:

    Location: _____

    Job Title/Description: _____

    Years Employed There: _____

Company Name:

    Location: _____

    Job Title/Description: _____

    Years Employed There: _____

PARENTS — MOTHER

Maiden Name: _____

First Name: _____

Middle Name: _____

Birth Date: _____

Birthplace: _____

If Applicable:

Death Date: _____

Cause of Death: _____

Place of Burial: _____

Location: _____

Lot#, Grave #, Marker or Monument info): _____

_____

PARENTS — FATHER

Last Name: _____

First Name: _____

Middle Name: _____

Birth Date: _____

Birthplace: _____

If Applicable:

Death Date: _____

Cause of Death: _____

Place of Burial: _____

Location: _____

Lot#, Grave #, Marker or Monument info): _____

_____

CHILDREN

Full Name: _____

Date of Birth: _____

Birthplace: _____

Current Residence: _____

Full Name: _____

Date of Birth: _____

Birthplace: _____

Current Residence: _____

Full Name: _____

Date of Birth: _____

Birthplace: _____

Current Residence: _____

IMPORTANT NAMES

Full Name: _____

Date of Birth: _____

Birthplace: _____

Current Residence: _____

Full Name: _____

Date of Birth: _____

Birthplace: _____

Current Residence: _____

Full Name: _____

Date of Birth: _____

Birthplace: _____

Current Residence: _____

GRANDPARENTS

What country did your ancestors come from?

_____

_____

_____

Why and when did they move here?

_____

_____

_____

Paternal Grandmother

Full Name: _____

Date of Birth: _____

Birthplace: _____

Current Residence: _____

IMPORTANT NAMES

Date of Death: _____

Cause of Death: _____

Place of Burial: _____

Location (Lot #, Grave #, Marker or Monument info):

_____

Fraternal Grandmother

Full Name: _____

Date of Birth: _____

Birthplace: _____

Current Residence: _____

Date of Death: _____

Cause of Death: _____

Place of Burial: _____

Location (Lot #, Grave #, Marker or Monument info):

_____

Paternal Grandfather

Full Name: _____

Date of Birth: _____

Birthplace: _____

Current Residence: _____

Date of Death: _____

Cause of Death: _____

Place of Burial: _____

Location (Lot #, Grave #, Marker or Monument info):

_____

Fraternal Grandfather

Full Name: _____

Date of Birth: _____

Birthplace: _____

Current Residence: _____

Date of Death: _____

Cause of Death: _____

Place of Burial: _____

Location (Lot #, Grave #, Marker or Monument info):

_____

MEDICAL HISTORY

The following is a list of known medical conditions/major injuries that should be noted:

Name of illness/injury:

Age of occurrence: _____

Type of treatment: _____

_____

_____

Long-term impact: _____

_____

_____

_____

Name of illness/injury:

Age of occurrence: _____

Type of treatment: _____

_____

_____

Long-term impact: _____

_____

_____

_____

Name of illness/injury:

Age of occurrence: _____

Type of treatment: _____

_____

_____

Long-term impact: _____

_____

_____

_____

Name of illness/injury:

Age of occurrence: _____

Type of treatment: _____

_____

_____

Long-term impact: _____

_____

_____

_____

Name of illness/injury:

Age of occurrence: _____

Type of treatment: _____

_____

_____

Long-term impact: _____

_____

_____

_____

Name of illness/injury:

Age of occurrence: _____

Type of treatment: _____

_____

_____

Long-term impact: _____

_____

_____

_____

Name of illness/injury:

Age of occurrence: _____

Type of treatment: _____

_____

_____

Long-term impact: _____

_____

_____

_____

FAMILY MEMORIES

What I know of my family's history prior to my birth:

IMPORTANT NAMES

Who most influenced my life (How?):

The one thing I did in my life that made me the happiest or most proud — my greatest accomplishment:

Advice or philosophy of life I want to pass on to my children and/or grandchildren:

Unique and memorable experiences I had in life.

Author's examples:

- Sat in the President's box at the Kennedy Center as guest of President Johnson.

- Lived in Fontainbleau, France.

- Travelled to Hawaii to meet husband on R&R from Vietnam.

- Sat next to the President of South Korea

- Meeting so many interesting people when my daughter Robin was co-host on TV's "Doubledare" on Nickelodeon.

WHO CARES

PART VIII
Financial and
Business Affairs

MY BUSINESS AFFAIRS

Locating and understanding where important papers can be found (provide location, contact person if needed, contact phone numbers):

Will:

Name _____

Phone _____

Address _____

_____

Trusts:

Location _____

Type _____

Name of Trustee _____

Phone _____

Address _____

_____

Checking Account(s):

Name_____

Phone _____

Address _____

_____

Account Number(s) _____

Savings Account(s):

Name_____

Phone _____

Address _____

_____

Account Number(s) _____

Stock Certificates:

Name_____

Phone _____

Address _____

_____

Owner's Name _____

FINANCES | BUSINESS

Stock Certificates (continued):

Name_____

Phone_____

Address_____

_____

Owner's Name _____

Name_____

Phone_____

Address_____

_____

Owner's Name _____

Name_____

Phone_____

Address_____

_____

Owner's Name _____

Bonds:

Name_____

Phone_____

Address_____

_____

Owner's Name_____

Insurance Policies (see page 174):

Special Collections
(i.e., stamps, coins, other collectables):

Item Name: _____

Name_____

Phone_____

Address _____

_____

Any Inheritance Due:

_____

FINANCES | BUSINESS

DISTRIBUTION OF ASSETS

NOTE: your will is the single best tool for delineating what items of value are to be distributed to which individual(s). The list below can serve as a backup tool. List here "Item" and name(s) of recipients. Be as specific as you can. Use additional paper as needed.

How I would like my loved ones to divide my furnishings, jewelry, etc.:

FINANCIAL AND BUSINESS AFFAIRS

☛ Make every effort to discourage arguments or disputes over personal property from wrecking family relations. Material items never take the place of love for one another.

IMPORTANT NAMES AND PHONE NUMBERS

Important Names and Phone Numbers (this list includes individuals you deal with both personally and for business):

Bank

Name _____

Phone _____

Address _____

_____

List all account numbers _____

_____

_____

_____

_____

Financial Planner

Name

Phone

Address

Lawyer

Name

Phone

Address

Accountant

Name

Phone

Address

Broker

Name

Phone

Address

Money Market Fund

Name

Phone

Address

Account Number(s)

Funeral Home

Name

Phone

Address

Safety Deposit Box/Keys

Name

Phone

Address

Box Number

Comments:

FINANCES | BUSINESS

WHERE TO LOCATE IMPORTANT PAPERS:

CREDIT CARDS:

Visa:

Account # _____

MasterCard:

Account # _____

Discover:

Account # _____

American Express:

Account # _____

Other Credit Cards:

Account # _____

Location/Comments:_____

_____

_____

_____

Bank Account Books:

Location/Comments:_____

_____

_____

_____

Rental Property Payment Books:

Location/Comments:_____

_____

_____

_____

FINANCES | BUSINESS

Other Financial Records:

Location/Comments: _____

_____

_____

_____

_____

IMPORTANT KEYS:

Keys to House/Apartment:

Location/Comments: _____

_____

Keys to Car(s):

Location/Comments: _____

_____

Other Important Keys:

Location/Comments: _____

_____

WILL:

Two people with copies of my will:

Name_____

Address_____

Phone #_____

Name_____

Address_____

Phone #_____

POWERS OF ATTORNEY

Two people with Powers of Attorney:

Name_____

Address_____

Phone #_____

Name_____

Address_____

Phone #_____

FINANCES | BUSINESS

BIRTH CERTFICATE:

Two people with copies of my birth certificate:

Name _____

Address _____

Phone # _____

Name _____

Address _____

Phone # _____

INSURANCE POLICIES (Including Long-Term Health):

Name of Insurance Company _____

Insurance Company Phone # _____

Policy # _____

Address of Company _____

_____

Location of Policy _____

Name of Insurance Company _____

Insurance Company Phone # _____

FINANCIAL AND BUSINESS AFFAIRS

Policy #_____

Address of Company _____

_____

Location of Policy _____

Name of Insurance Company _____

Insurance Company Phone #_____

Policy #_____

Address of Company _____

_____

Location of Policy _____

Cash or Long Term Care Policy that I have to cover nursing home costs:

Name of Policy _____

Policy # _____

Address of Carrier _____

Location of Policy _____

Name of Policy _____

Policy # _____

Address of Carrier _____

Location of Policy _____

Name of Policy _____

Policy # _____

Address of Carrier _____

Location of Policy _____

List of Personal Assets:

Name of Item _____

Location of Item _____

Appraisal _____

Location of Appraisal _____

Name of Item _____

Location of Item _____

Appraisal _____

Location of Appraisal _____

Name of Item _____

Location of Item _____

Appraisal _____

Location of Appraisal _____

Name of Item _____

Location of Item _____

Appraisal _____

Location of Appraisal _____

FINANCES | BUSINESS

Pensions and Retirement Accounts:

Title of Pension Plan/Retirement Account:

_____

Account Number: _____

Location: _____

_____

Title of Pension Plan/Retirement Account:

_____

Account Number: _____

Location: _____

_____

Title of Pension Plan/Retirement Account:

_____

Account Number: _____

Location: _____

_____

FINANCIAL AND BUSINESS AFFAIRS

Home:

Address: _____

Purchase Price: _____

Current Value: _____

Date of last appraisal: _____

Location of Deed(s): _____

Automobile(s):

Make/Model: _____

Year: _____

Location of Title: _____

Make/Model: _____

Year: _____

Location of Title: _____

Make/Model: _____

Year: _____

Location of Title: _____

Other Assets:

Furs

Comments: _____

_____

_____

Jewelry

Comments: _____

_____

_____

Antiques

Comments: _____

_____

_____

Stamps:

Comments: _____

_____

_____

Coins

Comments: _____

_____

_____

Other

Comments: _____

_____

_____

_____

_____

_____

_____

_____

_____

_____

_____

_____

FINANCES | BUSINESS

My Monthly Bills and Obligations:

Name	Total	Contact
Mortage		
Utilities		
Gas		
Water		
Electric		
Car Payment		
Insurance Premiums		
Regular Health-related		
Other		

Any Debts Owed:

Type: _____

Name to be paid: _____

Address: _____

Phone # _____

Type: _____

Name to be paid: _____

Address: _____

Phone # _____

PART IX
Life's Lessons

*What I have learned in life and
would like to pass on to everyone's loved ones.*

"My children are coming today. They mean well, but they worry. They think I should have a railing in the hall, a telephone in the kitchen. They want someone to come in when I take a bath. They don't really like my living alone. Help me to be grateful for their concern. And help them to understand that I have to do what I can as long as I can. They're right when they say there are risks. I might fall. I might leave the stove on. But there is no challenge, no possibility of triumph, no real aliveness without risk. When they were young and rode bicycles and climbed trees and went away to camp, I was terrified, but I let them go. Because to hold them would have been to hurt them. Now roles are reversed. Help them to see. Keep me from being grim or stubborn about it. But don't let them smother me."

— **Elise Maclay,** St. Cloud Visitor

REGRETS IN MY LIFE

If I had to do it all over again…

Regrets:

Special interests I wish I had pursued:

What is really important in life:

QUESTIONS ASKED OF SEVERAL PEOPLE
What Have You Learned Over Your Lifetime?

*Note: Most of the lessons learned (and remembered) listed below involve people not "things."

🐌 I've learned that I like my teacher because she cries when we sing *Silent Night*.

—Age 6

🐌 I've learned that our dog doesn't want to eat my broccoli either. —Age 7

I've learned that just when I get my room the way I like it; Mom makes me clean it up again. — Age 12

I've learned that if you want to cheer yourself up; you should try cheering someone else up. — Age 14

I've learned that although it's hard to admit it, I'm secretly glad my parents are strict with me. — Age 15

I've learned that silent company is often more healing than words of advice.
— Age 24

I've learned that brushing my child's hair is one of life's great pleasures. — Age 26

I've learned that there are people who love you dearly but just don't know how to show it. — Age 42

I've learned that you can make someone's day by simply sending them a little note. — Age 44

I've learned that children and grandparents are natural allies. — Age 47

I've learned that no matter what happens, or how bad it seems today, life goes on, and it will be better tomorrow. — Age 48

I've learned that singing *Amazing Grace* can lift my spirits for hours. — Age 49

- I've learned that you can tell a lot about a man by the way he handles these three things: a rainy day, lost luggage and tangled Christmas tree lights.

  — Age 52

- I've learned that regardless of your relationship with your parents, you miss them terribly after they die.

  — Age 53

- I've learned that making a living is not the same thing as making a life.

  — Age 58

- I've learned that life sometimes gives you a second chance.

  — Age 62

I've learned that if you pursue happiness, it will elude you. But if you focus on your family, the needs of others, your work, meeting new people, and doing the very best you can, happiness will find you. — Age 65

I've learned that whenever I decide something with kindness, I usually make the right decision. — Age 66

I've learned that everyone can use a prayer. — Age 72

I've learned that it pays to believe in miracles. And to tell the truth, I've seen several. — Age 75

I've learned that even when I have pains, I don't have to be one. — Age 82

I've learned that every day you should reach out and touch someone. People love a human touch, holding hands, a warm hug, or just a friendly pat on the back. — Age 85

I've learned that I still have a lot to learn. — Age 92

I've learned that you should pass this on to someone you care about. Sometimes they just need a little something to make them smile. — Ageless

— Anonymous

A MESSAGE TO THE READER

Dear Reader:

Hopefully, this guidebook will give you some ideas as to what lies ahead as you get older and dependent upon other human beings.

In this guide, I spoke of the nursing home and the impact it had on me. I have observed and have learned. I have met some warm, wonderful residents. They would prefer being home, but they know (most of them, that is) that they need additional help. I have also seen many unhappy, ornery older residents. I truly believe that people do not change that much. If he/she was unfriendly and hateful as a young person, that is the same type of person he/she will be as an older person, at home or in a nursing home.

I have written the following story based on a certain patient I met at a nursing home. Perhaps this story will drive home the point that you, as an independent, vital person must **evaluate your life** NOW. Where is your life heading? Will your later life be filled with love or loneliness? Are you taking time to nurture relationships? I contend, while you are young you must plan for your monetary security. But — and this is a big "BUT" — not at the expense of family and friends. Stay in contact and enjoy the important people in your life. It is not a sin to desire wealth — but it is pitiful when it means you have no time to love and enjoy family and friends.

A WASTED LIFE

My God, I *must be having a nightmare! What am I doing here? Who are these strangers? When did this happen to me? I was always in control of my own life. What went wrong? I don't like some of these awful odors!*

I hear myself yelling, "Nurse! Nurse! Help me!" A pretty person in a white uniform walks in and tells me to stop yelling. I want to know where I am. She pats me on the shoulder and says that I am in the Nursing Home. She tells me everything is going to be all right and that I will soon get used to where I am. I don't want to get used to where I am! I don't want to get used to this place! She tells me to relax. She will be right back to wash and dress me. I wait and wait. I doze off. I awaken and try to clear my head. I try to remember how I got here.

I remember tripping over a rug in my study and falling. I lay there in pain all night. I got cold and yelled. No one heard me. I lived alone. I couldn't reach the phone. I was divorced and not close to my children. I knew no one would be phoning to see how I was. I passed out. When I awakened I was in the hospital with a broken hip. My cleaning woman had found me in the morning and had called an ambulance. From the hospital, I was brought here.

I look around my room and see a wheelchair. Will I sit in it for the rest of my life? I hear a lot of activity and a lot of announcements. I lay there thinking — thinking — always thinking. Thinking makes me "clammy" all over. I don't want to think. People used to tell me how much they needed faith in their lives. Not me. I was in control and doing just fine. Look at me now. Who is in control now?

Would God listen and forgive my self-centered, self-ish life? Is it too late? Where is my family? Why hasn't anyone called?

What am I good for anymore? Nobody needs me. How "self-important" am I now? When I was young, I swore I would someday live in a beautiful home, have expensive cars and lots of money. I wanted the whole package. But where did all the power and money get me? All my "things" are now left behind. None of the prestige and wealth I craved can comfort me now. How stupid I was to crave for — what? I look around my room. I see a wheelchair, a dresser, a nightstand, a small TV, a chair, a sink, and a closet. That's it for "things" for me from now on. I look at the open doorway, hoping to see one familiar face. Why in heaven would I expect love and attention now? I never took time to give it.

Sure I had a wife and family, but they came second to my career. How could my children expect me to get away from work to see their plays and games? I was the "breadwinner!" How could they expect me to be home on time for dinner at night? I was the "breadwinner!" How could my wife not understand when I had to frequently cancel out on social engagements? I was the "breadwinner!" As a husband and father, I was out making a living. A wife and mother took care of the home and children. When did it happen? When did my wife and children finally leave me out of their lives? All of a sudden, I wasn't asked to join in much anymore. Their lives went on without me. Weren't they impressed with my success and power at work?

Throughout my life, I wanted to prove that I had made it. I wanted to be seen at the right places with the right people. Where are all these people — the "right people" — now? I am beginning to realize who the "right people" really were. My kind cleaning woman had so little yet managed to tolerate my tirades and remain patient. My neighbor, who was from another country and tried so hard to be my friend, but I wasn't interested. What could he do for me? Wrong nationality. Wrong profession. Now I realize that he was trying to give me something from his heart — his time and his attention. There was no ulterior motive. How I would love his friendship now! I looked down on so many people. I was so prejudiced and judgmental. It made me feel good to think that I was better than others — richer, smarter, right image. Better! Better! Better! Am I better now? A lonely, scared old man? If only I could go back. How much I lost in life by not getting to know so many nice people who crossed my path. Why did I let so much hate and prejudice get in my way? What a waste!

I'm sitting in the doorway of my room now just watching people. I see Joan — a crippled, bent over, old lady who tries so hard to smile and be

LIFE'S LESSONS

pleasant. Doesn't she know where she is? Why is it some people can adjust and make almost any situation **"okay?"** Joan has constant visitors. Her family visits often. People passing by her stop and give her a smile and a hug. Now who is wealthier? Me, with lots of money and almost no personal contact? Or Joan who is surrounded by sincere warmth from caring people? I can't buy that. I can't force that.

Why did I feel I always had to compete with my brother as an adult? Growing up we had been very close. Later on, I had little time for anything but work. We grew apart. Bob moved out of state. I heard his wife needed dental work and couldn't afford it. I heard he and his wife worked to make ends meet. I had heard my nieces and nephews worked their way through college. Why didn't I step in and help? Did I feel a little superior seeing them struggle? Did I want to prove my success by waiting for him to come to me and ask for help? Little *did I know I was measuring my success against his only by the total in my bank account. How short-sighted! I didn't see how many hours per day my brother put aside to attend his children's games and school activities. I never saw them all together, each night at dinner, laughing and sharing the day's events. I never saw the nights Bob and Mary were content being together watching TV. I hear he has a loving, growing family with a lot of happy memories surrounding him. Who won the "competition" between brothers? Who ended up wealthier?*

I wonder where my children are. Do they ever speak lovingly of me? Will they ever come to see me? Why hasn't anyone called? I always threatened them that at any point I could take them out of my will. Don't they care anymore? Why hasn't anyone called? Please God, don't let me die a lonely, fright-ened old man. Oh God, what have I done to myself?

TOP 10 PRIORITIES FOR CAREGIVERS

This list is adapted from the personal experiences of a caregiver.

1) LOVE

Remember if it Is your mother or father, no doubt, you love them. If you can do something to make him or her more comfortable, do it! Don't have regrets when they are gone.

2) ASSURANCE

Do your best and that is all anyone can ask of you. Don't compare notes with siblings, it only causes strife and tension.

3) PEACE OF MIND

If your loved one is in a nursing home, go at various times of the day to visit. This way you can see for yourself if your loved one Is being cared for adequately at all times.

4) COMFORT

Don't give "goodies" to a loved one in a nursing home when you arrive Give the "goodies" to them when you are leaving. By doing so, you see your loved one occupied and content when you are leaving.

5) INFORMATION

Find out the wishes and desires of the loved one you are caring for. Don't assume you know. Talk TO him/her, don't talk ACT him/her.

6) COMRADESHIP

Find a cherished friend or confidant to use as a sounding board. You are giving your time, efforts and love as a caregiver. Don't diminish your efforts by complaining to everyone you meet.

7) FAITH

If you are open to this, lean on your faith during a very trying time. My faith and hope truly pulled me through.

8) BALANCE

Take care of yourself. You NEED an outlet, if you are uptight and stressed, you will pass this onto your family and the loved one you are caring for.

9) KNOWLEDGE

Know that you are not alone during this trying time. Use the resources available, (i.e. Support groups, Online resources, Clergy, and other Caregivers.)

10) ACCEPTANCE

You are only one human being. You cannot make a person healthy or happy. ...you can only try to make him/her comfortable. When you have done all that you can, take time to give yourself a big hug!

GENERAL GUIDANCE FOR CAREGIVERS

I *do pray that when* I *am elderly...*}

- I will be kept clean.

- I will be fed nutritious meals.

- I will be helped to keep my dignity as much as possible.

- I will obtain necessary medical care.

- I will not be treated as though I am already dead. I hope I will have the opportunity to continue to be around things I love — family, friends, jokes, music, movies, and good food until the day I do die!!

- I hope to be remembered for the love and support I tried to give to my family and friends. To be loved in return is to have true wealth.

While I *am still* "rational," I *do realize that later on...*

- You cannot be with me 24 hours a day.

- You must go on with your life.

- You love me and will try to do your best to help keep me comfortable.

- At times, you will feel anger and guilt when I thrash out in frustration. I am not angry with you. I am angry and frustrated that I have become helpless and older.

- You did not make me older or sick.

- You must take care of your family and yourself. Don't feel guilty when you cannot be with me. Go on with your life.

Signed: _____

(Your signature here)

NOTE TO MY CAREGIVERS
Things I learned
When I was a Caregiver

SINCE YOU ARE THE ONE who will be in need of care in the future, feel free to add anything you feel appropriate. If you disagree with something, cross it out. This guide must become "your guide."

If you have brothers or sisters, **do not** expect every one of them to take care of your parent in the same way. Each person has to live with his/her own decisions. Each should pretend he/she is **an only child**. Do not compare notes about what each one is doing or not doing. It only leads to anger, family

LIFE'S LESSONS

strife and illness. You do what you can — with love.

Do not look for praise or condemnation. It is to God that you have to answer. If you truly believe you are doing your share to help care and give your loved one love and kindness, so be it.

It is so much easier to care for a loved one when everyone **cooperates**. Talk together. Plan together. Just don't compare!

When you visit an elderly person, give him/her your **undivided attention**. Do not always look rushed and frustrated. Sometime you might be the only visitor he/she sees for days. A hug, kiss and sincere smile means so much. Sit close and hold his/her hand. **Show** the love you feel.

Before each visit, take a minute to visualize yourself in the condition and environment. What would be **your** physical and emotional needs?

Do not **talk down** to the person for whom you are providing care.

Take the person out of their environment as much as possible. Let him/her feel alive. A mall is a great place to go. (People to watch, varieties of food, accommodations for wheelchairs, and bathrooms are accessible.) Such small "outings" will let the person know his/her "confinement" will not be continuous.

If possible, bring a favorite food when you visit. (I find that elderly people talk among themselves about food, ailments and constipation! Wouldn't you rather they talked about food?) For an extra special treat, set a pretty table with flowers, etc. Bring an up-to-date album to show the latest family pictures.

I always try to remember what a friend, Sister Jo Anne, said to me. "Dee, you did not make your mother old, and you did not make her sick. You can love her and try to make her life as comfortable as possible, but you cannot make her young and happy. You are not God."

Carry a comb, makeup, nail polish, etc. with you if you are visiting an elderly female. My Mother loved to look nice like we all do. Remember that he/she is elderly, not dead! If the person you are visiting is male, why not surprise him with his favorite aftershave or cologne?

Before I would leave, I always handed my Mom a newspaper, magazine or something I knew she enjoyed. That way, she had something to look forward to when I left. Leave with a big hug and a promise to return.

Each time I would leave, I told my Mom something she could look forward to when I came back. "Mom, Tuesday we will visit Peggy. Mom, I am bringing Alice to visit with you on Thursday. Mom, I am taking you to the shore on Monday and Tuesday." Everyone needs a reason to go on living.

Someone once told me to put cotton in my ears, Vaseline on my glasses, and heavy gloves on my hands and combat boots on my feet. This will give you some idea of how an elderly person sees, hears, and feels.

Remember that we are all aging. Treat your loved one the way you would want to be treated.

Do not kid yourself into thinking your own children are not watching. They are observing how lovingly you treat your Mom and Dad or other family members. More often than not, that is the way you will be treated someday.

Be fair, loving, kind, and compassionate. Keep calm, but stay in control.

IDEAS AND GIFTS TO HELP THE ELDERLY

- To pay bills or run errands for your care recipient, have him/her put all bills and list of needs into one box. You can pick these up when you visit.

- Leave a few dollars so that a pizza can be ordered or some other special treat. (Some patients met as a group and did this weekly in the nursing home.)

- If the person is in a wheelchair, clip a portable digital phone to the chair. (Purchase one that has 1-button-dialing for often-used numbers.)

- Purchase a clock with large numerals for the wall.

- Purchase a calendar with large squares and fill in important family dates: birthdays, anniversaries, etc.

- Purchase a bulletin board and attach recent pictures of the family.

- Frame and hang a picture of the care recipient over his/her bed. A picture taken when he/she was young and vibrant. (It made my Mom so proud each time someone said how beautiful she was.)

- Check and see that he/she has an adequate supply of allowed snacks.

- Purchase a radio and put it on a station he/she likes to listen to. (Then, only the "ON"/ "OFF" knob had to be turned to "ON.")

- Purchase a beautiful notebook for visitors to sign. (This even helps the caregiver to check on who has been in for a visit.)

- Foster closeness by giving your loved one a weekly manicure. It provides "private time" to talk and to make personal contact with one another.

- If your care recipient is living at home alone, make certain all medicines can easily be opened. Write out IN BIG LETTERS the quantities and times each medication must be taken.

- Help remove facial hair — this is a constant worry.

- Make certain hair is always washed and well groomed.

- Do not visit at the same time if your loved one is in a nursing home. Check in at different and varied times to make certain your loved one is getting proper care all day long — not just during anticipated visits.

CONCLUSION

To the Reader:

Always remember this quotation:

The opposite of Love is not Hate — but Indifference.

People filling out this book to help make their loved ones' lives a little easier are certainly not "Indifferent."

God Bless and Good Luck!

Dee Marrella

RED ALERT

Note: Take a half dozen sheets of 81/2" x 11" blank paper and recreate the **RED ALERT** list found on the next two pages. Fill out the **RED ALERT** sheets completely, fold them and place them in the rear of this guide book so that the top of the sheet and the words **RED ALERT** can be easily seen. The words **RED ALERT** should be visible above the pages of the book and to anyone who finds this book. The information on this **RED ALERT** is _**critical**_ information that you would want anyone who found you to have quick access.

On this page I am listing **Very Important** information about myself. Please refer to it when any emergency situation arises.

In Case of Emergency

Key person to Contact

Name: _____

Address: _____

Telephone # (Office): _____

Telephone # (Home): _____

Phone Numbers of Relatives:

Name: _____

Relationship: _____

Telephone # : _____

Name: _____

Relationship: _____

Telephone # : _____

Name: _____

Relationship: _____

Telephone # : _____

Name: _____

Relationship: _____

Telephone # : _____

Name: _____

Relationship: _____

Telephone # : _____

Name: _____

Relationship: _____

Telephone # : _____

LIFE'S LESSONS

My Birth date and current age: _____

I am allergic to the following drugs:

_____

_____

_____

_____

I am allergic to the following foods:

_____

_____

_____

I AM being treated for (fill in with illness, condition, disease, i.e, Diabetes): _____

_____

_____

_____

_____

LIFE'S LESSONS

My Personal Physician is:

Name: _____

Address: _____

Telephone #: _____

My Pharmacy is:

Name: _____

Address: _____

Telephone #: _____

NOTE: Create these **RED ALERT** forms and have them ready for use at any time. Keep the most current version of this form folded with the **RED ALERT** facing out and inserted into the back of this guide.

PART X

*Words & Phrases
to Keep Handy*

A

Acute Care

Special care that is provided typically for a brief period of time to treat a certain illness or condition. This type of care often includes short-term hospital stays, doctor's visits, surgery, and X-rays.

Adult Care Home

A residence that offers services of a housing and personal care nature for 3 up to 16 residents. The owner or manager usually provides services such as meals, supervision, and transportation. Can also be known as a board and care home or group home.

Advance Directive for Health Care

Legal document, such as a living will, a durable power of attorney for healthcare, or both), prepared ahead of time and signed by a living and competent person in order to provide guidance for medical and health-care decisions (includ-ing the termination of life support and organ donation) in the event that he or she becomes incompetent to make such decisions.

Alzheimer's Disease

A progressive, irreversible disease of unknown cause that is the most common form of dementia, marked by the loss of cognitive ability (due to degeneration of the brain cells and serve loss of memory). It usually starts in late middle age or in old age as a loss of memory of recent events, which spreads to memories for more distant events. It progresses on average over the course of five to ten or fifteen years to a profound intellectual decline characterized by dementia and personal helplessness.

Assisted Living Facility

Often licensed and known as residential care facilities or rest homes, a residence that combines housing, supportive services, personalized assistance and healthcare designed to meet the individual's needs on a daily basis emphasizing residents' privacy and choice. These needs may include bathing, dressing, balancing a checkbook, medication reminders, and/or Housework for example. In many assisted living facilities, 24-hour supportive services are available to meet the planned and unplanned needs of the residents. These settings in which services are delivered may include self-contained apartment units or single or shared room units with private or area baths. Assisted Living Facilities can be similar to a Board and Care Home, but are typically larger.

Assistive Devices

A range of products designed to help elders or people with disabilities lead more independent lives. Examples include walking aids, motorized wheelchairs, lifts, raised/elevated toilet seats, bathtub seats, ramps, and handrails for example. In some cases, modifications to the living facility are required in order to properly utilize the devices. Also known as Architectural Adaptations, these are structural fabrications or remodeling in the home, work site, or other areas (including for example ramps, lifts, lighting, kitchen remodeling, bathroom adaptations) that remove or reduce physical barriers for an individual with a disability.

B

Beneficiary

A person or entity (perhaps a charity or estate) that receives a benefit or proceeds from something, a person or entity named or otherwise entitled to receive the proceeds (principal or income or both) from a will, trust, insurance policy, retirement plan, annuity or other contract. An individual covered by Medicare is also called a beneficiary.

Benefit Trigger

Before benefits are paid, certain benefit triggers and other conditions must be met. A benefit trigger is usually met by measuring a person's ability to do one or more activities of daily living (ADLs), such as bathing or dressing, or by testing the person's cognitive abilities. Also, it is a condition that must exist in order for an insurance company to pay benefits under a long-term care insurance policy. Benefits are triggered for nursing home care, assisted living, or home care when a person can't do two of the ADLs listed in the policy, or when a person has an obvious cognitive impairment like Alzheimer's and has met other conditions in the policy. Tax-qualified policies use a list of six ADLs: Bathing, Dressing, Transferring, Eating, Toileting, and Continence

Non-tax qualified policies use seven ADLs, adding ambulating (walking) to the list.

Benefits

A monetary sum or payment made or an entitlement available in accordance with an insurance policy or a public assistance program, or to someone else, such as a health care provider, to whom the insured person has assigned the benefits.

Board and Care Home

A Board and Care Home usually offers seniors supervision and some personal care (such as meals and transportation), but few onsite medical services. A small number of residents live (between 3 and 16) in a group home, sometimes in a refurbished single-family home. A Board and Care Home can be the same as an Assisted Living Facility, but on a smaller scale.

C

Care/Case Management

Care management is a coordinated care function (single point of entry) incorporating case finding, assessment, care planning, negotiation, care plan implementation, monitoring, and advocacy to assist clients and their families with complex needs in obtaining appropriate services. This program (operated privately or through social service agencies or public programs) locates, mobilizes and manages a variety of home care and other services needed by a frail elderly person at risk of nursing home placement. An assessment is performed to identify needs, and appropriate services are secured to enable the individual to remain at home. Case managers assist in gaining access to needed services for those persons eligible. They monitor the provision of these services as well as initiate and oversee the assessment and reassessment of an individual's level and plan of care.

Care Manager

A health care professional, typically a nurse or social worker, who arranges, monitors, or coordinates long-term care services. A care manager may also assess a patient's needs and develop a plan of care, subject to approval by the patient's physician. They may also be referred to as a care coordinator or case manager.

Chore Services

In short, they are assistance with chores such as home repairs, yard work, and heavy housecleaning. They are non-continuous household maintenance tasks intended to increase the safety of the individual(s) in their residence(s). Typically these tasks are limited to the following: replacing light bulbs, fuses, electric plugs and frayed cords, door locks, window catches, water pipes, faucets and/or washers. They can include installation and repair of safety equipment, screens and storm windows, weather stripping around doors, window shades and curtain rods. Furniture repair, the cleaning of appliances, rugs, basements and attics to remove potential hazards are included. As are washing walls and windows, scrubbing floors, pest control, mowing grass and raking leaves, clearing ice, snow, and leaves from sidewalks, driveways, and step, and trimming overhanging branches.

Chronically Ill Individual

A chronically ill individual, as defined by the federal government, is someone who has been certified (at least in the past twelve months) by a licensed health care practitioner as – (1) Being unable to perform, without substantial assistance from another individual, at least two daily living activities (eating, toileting, transferring, bathing, dressing, and continence) for at least 90 days due to a loss of functional capacity or (2) Requiring substantial supervision to protect the individual from threats to health and safety due to severe cognitive impairment.

Chronic Illness or Condition

There are two types of illnesses: acute and chronic. Acute illnesses (like a cold or the flu) are usually over relatively quickly. Chronic illnesses, though, are long-lasting health conditions (the word "chronic" comes from

the Greek word chronos, meaning time). An illness or other condition with one or more of the following characteristics: permanency, residual disability, requires rehabilitation training, or requires a long period of supervision, observation, or care. Typically, it is a disease or condition that lasts over a long period of time and cannot be cured; it is often associated with disability.

Codicil

A supplement, appendix, or legal change to a will.

Congregate Housing

Congregate (or supported) housing is a group housing option (such as individual apartments) for the elderly and disabled, with private living quarters and common dining and social areas with additional safety measures such as emergency call buttons. Support services vary, but usually include meals, housekeeping and activities. People living in a congregate housing facility require little or no personal care assistance.

Continuing Care Retirement Community (CCRC)

A are privately owned privately owned retirement community for people who cannot or who prefer not to maintain an independent household because they need some kind of long-term assistance or medical care that offer a broad range of services and degrees or levels of care based on individual needs. Also known as life care, these communities can range from full-time care in nursing homes to assisted living to independent living situations. It is not unusual for continuing care retirement communities (CCRCs) to be expensive and entry fees or payments required prior to acceptance along with continuing monthly fees.

Custodial Care

Room and board in a nursing home where assistance with activities of daily living is provided such as bathing, dressing, eating, and other non-medical care that most people do themselves. Medicare does not pay for custodial care. Medicaid provides the majority of reimbursement for custodial care, although very little. It is important to note that it is typical that individuals without professional training may provide this type of care.

D

Dementia

Dementia is a progressive brain dysfunction that leads to a gradually increasing restriction of daily activities, the deterioration of intellectual abilities such as vocabulary, abstract thinking, judgment, memory loss, and physical coordination. Alzheimer's disease is the best-known type of dementia. Dementia seriously affects patients as well as those around them. Most patients eventually require care in the long-term. Some degenerative diseases, vascular diseases or stroke, metabolic disorders, drugs and

WORDS & PHRASES

alcohol, and psychiatric disorders can cause dementia.

Depression

Depression is an illness that affects both mind and body—one that can make it difficult to handle everyday life. It is one of the most undiagnosed conditions among seniors. Research has linked depression to an imbalance in two of the naturally occurring chemicals in the brain and body, serotonin and norepinephrine. These chemicals help regulate how your body perceives thoughts and feelings—including pain. While people with a family history of depression may be more prone to the disease, anyone can become depressed. Sometimes the triggers are external—for example, relationship troubles or financial problems; at other times the disease can be brought about by physical illness or hormonal shifts. Depression can also occur without any identifiable trigger at all. Symptoms can include a persistent sad, anxious or "empty" mood, loss of interest or pleasure in activities once enjoyed and difficulty sleeping.

Discharge Planner

A health care professional or social worker who assists hospital patients and their families in transitioning from the hospital to another level of care such as a rehabilitation center, rehabilitation in a skilled nursing facility, home health care in the patient's home, or long-term care in a nursing home.

Do Not Resuscitate Order

A code or order usually appearing in a patient's medical record indicating that in the event the heart and/or breathing stops, no intervention be undertaken by staff. Death occurs undisturbed. This does not mean that the individual does not receive care. Continuing care is provided as it would to any individual (medications for pain, antibiotics, etc.) except as stated above.

Durable Medical Equipment

Known as DME (also known as Home Medical Equipment), this is equipment that: can be used over and over again, is ordinarily used for medical purposes, and is generally not useful to a person who isn't sick, injured or disabled. Initially, it is medical equipment ordered by a doctor who writes a prescription for it for use in the home. Equipment includes canes, crutches, walkers, hospital beds, wheelchairs, lifts, and prosthetics used at home. DME may be covered by Medicaid and in part by Medicare or private insurance.

E

Elder Care

A relatively new and growing area of health care that is concerned with providing medical and other services for the rapidly growing, aging population – typically persons 65 and older. It consists of a wide range of services provided at home, throughout the community, and in residential care facilities, which includes assisted living facilities and nursing homes. It can include such health-related services as rehabilitative therapies, skilled nursing, and palliative care. It also includes supervision and a wide range of supportive personal care and social services. Elder care is usually provided over an extended period of time to individuals needing the assistance of others to perform normal daily living activities due to cognitive impairment or loss of muscular strength or control. Typically Medicare does not cover the majority of elder care because it is viewed as custodial care.

Estate

The whole of one's possessions, especially all the property and debts left by one at death.

Executor

The person or institution appointed by a court or testator to execute his will, or to see its provisions carried into effect, after his decease.

the same job upon returning from FMLA leave.

F

Fiduciary

A person, such as a trustee or guardian, who holds assets of another person or beneficiary, often with the legal authority and duty to make decisions regarding financial matters on behalf of the other party. It is illegal for a fiduciary to misappropriate money for personal gain.

Family Medical Leave Act

Known as FMLA, the Federal law that requires any firm with over 50 employees to grant an eligible employee up to a total of 12 work weeks of unpaid leave during any 12-month period to care for a family member with a serious health condition – such as a senior. The employer must maintain an employee's group health insurance benefits while taking FMLA leave and must reinstate the employee in

G

Geriatric Care Manager

Geriatric Care Managers provide a variety of services for seniors and caregivers including assessment, planning and management of home and health care for seniors. Also known as senior care managers, a geriatric care manager generally conducts an interview and provides a home assessment before creating a senior care plan with recommendations.

Geriatrician

A geriatrician is a doctor who specializes in care for people 65 and older, caring for the special and changing needs of seniors. Geriatricians approach each patient's needs individually, and possess the knowledge and expertise needed to accommodate complex medical and social concerns.

Guardian

One who is legally responsible (appointed by a court) for the care and management of the person or property of an individual who is unable to take care of himself or herself.

H

Health Maintenance Organization

Known as an HMO, group insurance that entitles members to services of participating hospitals, clinics and physicians. For those aged 65 and older, a type of Medicare managed care plan where a group of doctors, hospitals and other health care providers agree to give health care to Medicare beneficiaries for a pre-established amount of money from Medicare every month. Typically members must get all of their care from the providers who participate in the plan. Use of providers outside the HMO, will require payment out of pocket for services.

Heir

Someone who inherits assets from an estate of another person who has died. The heir does not have to pay income tax or estate tax on the value of the inheritance received.

Home Care

Caring for an aging or impaired person in their home by providing homemaking, meal preparation, shopping, transportation and assistance with activities of daily living.

Home Care Aides

Individuals who provide nonmedical assistance to impaired individuals in their homes.

Home Health Agency (HHA)

Also known as an HHA, this is a public or private operation providing home health services which are supervised by a licensed health professional in the patient's home either directly or through arrangements with other organizations.

Home Health Care

Generally, home health services are initiated when an individual is no longer able to care for him or herself due to serious changes in their health. It is not unusual for a doctor, nurse, hospital discharge planner or case manager to suggest that professional help in the home, as an alternative to hospitalization or a nursing home, to assist with health care needs on a round-the-clock basis — although home health care services are usually provided on a visit basis rather than an hourly basis. Readmission to a hospital can often be prevented or delayed. Most services must be ordered by a physician, and must be medically necessary to maintain or improve your health condition, in order to be covered by health insurance. Home health care services are usually provided on a visit basis rather than an hourly basis.

Homebound

An individual is understood to be homebound if absences from the home are infrequent or of relatively short duration, or are attributable to the need to receive medical treatment. Leaving home to receive medical treatment includes going to adult day care so long as the individual receives therapeutic, psychosocial or medical treatment from a licensed or state-certified adult day-care facility. Any absence for a religious service is considered an absence of short duration and doesn't negate the homebound status.

Hospice and Hospice Care

This is a program providing palliative care that improves the quality of life of patients facing terminal illness (end-of-life) and their families. The prevention and relief of suffering by means of early identification and impeccable assessment and treatment of pain and other problems, physical, psychosocial and spiritual is all part of the program. Hospices 1) provide relief from pain and other distressing symptoms, 2) affirm life and regard dying as a normal process, 3) neither hasten or postpone death intentionally, 4) integrate both psychological and spiritual aspects of patient care, 5) offer a support system to help patients live as actively as possible until death, 6) offer a support system to help the family cope during the patient's illness and through bereavement, 7) use a team approach to address the needs of patients and their families, including bereavement counseling, when needed, (8) are designed to enhance quality of life, and may also positively influence the course of an illness, and 9) are applicable early in the course of illness, in conjunction with other therapies that are intended to prolong life, such as radiation or chemotherapy, and includes those investigations needed to better understand and manage distressing clinical complications. Hospice care can be provided at home, in a facility with a homelike setting, a hospital or a nursing home. The care includes physical care, counseling and support services, but

does not attempt to cure any illness.

I

Independent Living Facility

A type of living arrangement in which personal care services such as meals, housekeeping, transportation, and assistance with activities of daily living are available as needed to people who still live on their own in a residential facility. In most cases, the "assisted living" residents pay a regular monthly rent. They typically pay additional fees for the services they get.

Instrumental Activities of Daily Living

Instrumental activities of daily living (also known as IADLs) are activities related to independent living (without the assistance or substantial supervision of another person) and include for example grocery shopping and preparing meals, managing money, shopping for groceries or personal items, performing light or heavy housework, doing laundry, using a telephone, paying bills, and taking daily medications. Most long-term care insurance policies will not pay benefits for the loss of ability to perform IADLs.

Intermediate Care

Needed for people in stable condition who require daily care, but not round-the clock nursing supervision. Typically ordered by a doctor and supervised by registered nurses. Intermediate care is less specialized than skilled nursing care and it usually involves more personal care.

Intermediate care is generally needed for a long period of time.

Intermediate Care Facility

Nursing homes most frequently come to mind when people envision what is in reality an intermediate care facility (also known as an ICF). Recognized under the Medicaid program, they provides health-related care and services to individuals who do not require acute or skilled nursing care, but who, because of their mental or physical condition, require care and services above the level of room and board available only through facility placement. These facilities often have more mobile, less acutely ill residents than a skilled nursing facility, which provides sophisticated medical care to people with acute medical needs. An ICF is staffed by a team of nurses under the supervision of an attending physician. Much of the care provided in an ICF-- often called "custodial" or "maintenance care" and provided in large part by nurses' aides--is personal care like help with bathing, dressing, and eating. An ICF is often set up as a wing of a skilled nursing facility. Specific requirements for ICF's vary by state. Institutions for care of the mentally retarded or people with related conditions (ICF/MR) are also included. The distinction between "health-related care and services" and "room and board" is important since ICF's are subject to different regulations and coverage requirements than institutions that do not provide health-related care and services.

J

Joint Tenancy with Right of Survivorship

Ownership of property by two or more people in which the survivors automatically gain ownership of a decedent's interest. Upon the death of any joint tenant, his or her ownership interest automatically passes to the surviving joint tenant.

L

Level of Care

Known as LOC, an assessment of the type of care necessary to meet the individual needs of the client and their eligibility for programs and services. The assessment takes into consideration the client's needs in all aspects of development, level of functioning (levels include: protective, intermediate, and skilled), and potential to benefit from a particular program.

Life Care Plan

Specific plan developed by a professional known as a Life Care Planner. An important tool in the future of a catastrophically injured person (such as on the job, in a serious accident, through medical malpractice). The Life Care Planner summarizes the medical, educational, vocational, psychosocial, and daily living needs of the individual who can function indefinitely only with professional assistance. The Life Care Planner projects the long-term costs of care, and establishes rehabilitative goals while coordinating future care providers in order to best assure a continued recovery.

Living Trust

A trust created for and individual (the trustor) and administered by another party during the trustor's lifetime. The living trust may be formed because the trustor is either incapable of managing or unwilling to manage his or her assets. The trust can be revocable or irrevocable, depending upon the trustor's wishes. It avoids probate and assests are distributed typically faster than through a will. Also called an inter vivos trust.

Living Will

A legal document (a will) in which the signer requests not to be kept alive by medical life-support systems in the event of a terminal illness or incapacity..

Long-Term Care

Term used to represent a range of services that address the health, social, and personal care needs of individuals delivered over a long period of time to persons who have never developed or have lost some capacity for self care.

Long-Term Care Insurance

An insurance policy that provides benefits for the chronically ill or disabled over a long period of time that helps pay for some long-term medical and non-medical care, such as help with activities of daily living. Medicare typically does not pay for long-term care.

M

Managed Care

A system of health care that combines delivery and payment; and influences utilization of services, by employing management techniques designed to promote the delivery of cost-effective health care. Organizations created included MNOs, PPOs, and PSOs. Members pay a pre-established monthly amount for care to be provided regardless of the amount required.

Medicaid

Health care for the aged administered by the federal and state governments. A program dependent upon low level of income and assets relative to high level of medical/health care bills. Coverage and eligibility requirements vary from state-to-state. The primary payer of nursing home care. Some states offer home and community-based long-term care services for eligible individuals through their individual programs and are at the option of those states and are not mandated by federal law.

Medicare

A program under the U.S. Social Security Administration that reimburses hospitals and physicians for medical care provided to qualifying people over 65 years and to some younger people who are very ill or disabled. Benefits for nursing home and short-term home health services are limited and are generally available only to people while they are recovering from an acute illness. Coverage is restricted to medical care, and does not include prescription drugs or custodial care at home or in nursing homes.

Medicare HMOs

An HMO (Health Maintenance Organization) is a health plan that is also involved in how an individual's health care is delivered. Managed care refers to health plans coordinating one's health care with the individual and the providers that participate in the health plan. HMOs are the most common type of managed care. A Medicare HMO is an HMO that has contracted with the federal government under the Medicare+ Choice program to provide health benefits to individuals eligible for Medicare that choose to enroll in the HMO, instead of receiving their benefits and care through the traditional fee for service Medicare program. Members pay their regular monthly premiums to Medicare, and Medicare pays the HMO a fixed sum of money each month to provide Medicare benefits (such as hospitalization, doctor's visits, etc.). Medicare HMOs may provide extra benefits over and above regular Medicare benefits (such as prescription drug coverage, eyeglasses, etc.). Members do not pay Medicare deductibles and co-payments; however, the HMO may require them to pay an additional monthly premium and co-payments for some services. If members use providers outside the HMO's network, they pay the entire bill themselves unless the plan has a point of service option.

Medicare Supplement Insurance

Medicare supplement insurance helps pay expenses not covered by original Medicare (often referred to as MedSupp), such as deductibles and coinsurance and was designed to fill in the gaps left by Medicare.. However, non-covered charges will be the insured's responsibility. Policies that meet the definition of Medicare supplement insurance are clearly labeled, usually on the policy's front cover. May pay for some limited long-term care expenses, depending on the benefits package purchased. Also called Medigap.

Medical Power of Attorney

An advance directive with written instructions that appoint someone to make decisions about an individual's medical care.

N

Nursing Home

Filling a special niche in health care, a private facility that provides living quarters and care for the elderly or the chronically ill who do not need the intensive, acute care of a hospital but for whom remaining home is no longer appropriate. Licensed by the state, it offers residents personal care as well as skilled nursing care on a 24-hour basis. Nursing homes are capable of caring for individuals with a wide range of medical conditions. Provides nursing care, personal care, room and board, supervision, medication, therapies and rehabilitation.

Nursing homes come in different sizes and with different names. They may also be known as: health centers, havens or manors, homes for the aged, nursing homes or centers, care centers, continuing care centers, living centers, or convalescent centers.

Nurse Practitioner

Known as an NP, a registered nurse working in an expanded nursing role, usually with a focus on meeting primary health care needs. They conduct physical examinations, interpret laboratory results, select plans of treatment, identify medication requirements, and perform certain medical management activities for selected health conditions. Some specialize in geriatric care.

O

Ombudsman

A representative who investigates complaints and mediates fair settlements for a public agency or a private nonprofit, especially between aggrieved parties such as older consumers who reside in long-term care

facilities and the facility, institution or organization.

Outpatient

A patient who does not reside in or has not been admitted to the hospital where they are being treated and receiving ambulatory care.

P

Personal Emergency Response System

In case of a fall or other medical emergency, An electronic device enables the user to contact assistance 24-hours-a-day simply by pressing a button in the event of an emergency (personal medical issue, a fall, fire, etc.)

Physician Assistant

A specially trained and licensed or otherwise credentialed individual who performs tasks under the direction of a supervising physician which might otherwise be performed by a physician. Usually called a PA.

Plan of Care

A written plan describing what specific services and care needed for an individual's health problem. An individual's plan of care must be prepared or approved by their doctor.

Point-of-Service Plan

A health plan that allows members to choose to receive services from a participating or non-participating network provider, usually with a financial disincentive for going outside the network. More of a product than an organization, POS plans can be offered by HMOs, PPOs, or self-insured employers.

Power of Attorney

A General Power of Attorney is a legal document which gives the person you choose (the agent) the power to manage your assets and financial affairs while you are alive. The simplest and least expensive legal device for authorizing a person to manage the affairs of another. The document must be signed by an individual (the principal) while that person has the required legal capacity to give their agent clear and concise instructions. The appointment may be for a fixed period and can be revoked by the individual at any time providing he or she still has the legal capacity to do so. A power of attorney ceases when the individual dies. The executor named in your will then takes over the responsibilities of your estate.

A Durable Power of Attorney stays valid even if you become unable to handle your own affairs (incapacitated). If you don't specify that you want your power of attorney to be durable, it will automatically end if you later become incapacitated

A Limited Power of Attorney allows the principal to give only specific powers to the agent. The limited power of attorney is used to allow the agent to handle specific matters when the principal is unavailable or unable to do so.

Forms needed for specific states may be found at:

http://www.uslegalforms.com/power-atty.htm.

Power of Attorney for Health Care

Allows an individual to appoint a person to make medical decisions for them in the event they are unable to do so for themselves. A written legal document in which one person (the principal) appoints another person to make health care decisions on behalf of the principal in the event the principal becomes incapacitated (the document defines incapacitation). This instrument can contain instructions about specific medical treatment that should be applied or withheld. While its purpose remains essentially the same from state-to-state, the name of this document can vary; for example, in Florida it is called a Designation of Health Care Surrogate.

Forms needed for specific states may be found at: *http://www.uslegalforms.com/power-atty.htm.*

Preferred Provider Organization

A type of managed care plan (known as a PPO). Members have a choice of utilizing healthcare providers in the PPO network, or hospitals, doctors and other healthcare professionals outside the plan for an additional cost.

Primary Care Physician

Physician responsible for a person's general or basic health care (known as General Practitioner or Family Doctor). The physician an individual sees first for most health problems. They make sure you get the care needed to stay healthy. They might talk with other more specialized doctors and healthcare providers and make a referral to them. In many Medicare managed care plans, participants must see their primary care doctor before seeing other healthcare providers.

Primary Caregiver

The individual or individuals, usually the spouse or adult

child, over the age of eighteen years designated by a qualified patient who has consistently assumed responsibility for the housing, health or safety of that qualified patient on a day-by-day basis. They take responsibility for caring for the physical, psychological and social needs of another individual.

Probate

Proof that a will is valid and that its terms are being carried out. Probate is accomplished by an executor/executrix (if a will exists) who is paid a fee based on the size of the estate that passes through the will. Certain trusts and jointly owned property pass to beneficiaries without being subject to probate and the attendant fee. Executor or a court-appointed administrator (if there is no will), manages and distributes a decedent's property to heirs and/or beneficiaries.

Provider

A person or organization who helps in identifying or prevent-

ing or treating illness and/or disability.

These can be any of the following: a properly-licensed doctor, health care professional, hospital, or other health care facility, including a home health agency, that provides health care or related social services.

Provider Sponsored Organization

Similar to an HMO or Medicare HMO except that this managed care organization (known as a PSO) is owned by the providers in that plan and these providers share the financial risk assumed by the organization.

R

Rehabilitation Services

Services designed to improve/restore a person's functioning; includes physical therapy, occupational therapy, and/or speech therapy. May be provided at home or in long-term care facilities. May be covered in part by Medicare.

Because rehabilitation services are an optional Medicaid benefit, not all states provide this service.

Residential Care

Room, board and personal care provided in a fashion that falls between the nursing care delivered in skilled and intermediate care facilities and the assistance provided through social services. Typically 24-hour supervision is provided to individuals requiring assistance with daily living activities.

Residential Care Facility

Generic term for group homes, specialized apartment complexes, or other institutions providing care services (room, board and personal care) for residents. The term is used to refer to a range of residential care options including assisted living facilities, board and care homes and skilled nursing facilities providing 24-hour supervision of individuals who, because of old age or impairments, necessarily need assistance with the activities of daily living.

Respite

The in-home care of a chronically ill beneficiary intended to give the caregiver a rest. Can also be provided by a hospice or a nursing facility.

Respite Care

Includes any temporary service which lets caregivers take a break from caring for people with disabilities, illnesses, dementia or other health problems while a third party assumes the regular caregiver's role. Types of respite include having someone come into the home so that the caregiver can relax or run errands; providing out-of-home respite through adult day programs for the impaired relative; and/or extending overnight respite opportunities (in-home or out-of-home) so that the caregiver can extend relief.

S

Senior Care Manager

Also known as case managers or geriatric care managers, these professionals (social workers, nurses, gerontologists or other professionals trained to work as care managers with older adults) provide on-going services such as coordinating all aspects of the elder's care with the client, family, doctor and service providers. Services also includes in-home assessments, written plans of care, and initiating and regular monitoring of services being provided to the elder. Some care management agencies provide additional services such as transportation or 24 hour on-call nursing care. They may offer conservatorship and/or guardianship when requested and decreed necessary by a District Court. Payment may come from private, special project, grant or governmental funds

Skilled Care

Institutional care (a subset of post-acute care) that is less intensive than hospital care in its nursing and medical service, but which includes procedures whose administration requires the training and skills of an RN. This care is usually needed 24 hours a day, must be ordered by a physician, and must follow a plan of care. Individuals usually get skilled care in a nursing home but may also receive it in other places. "Higher level" of care (such as injections, catheterizations, and dressing changes) provided by trained medical professionals, including nurses, doctors, and physical therapist. Both Medicare and Medicaid reimburse for care at the skilled level. Medicare reimburses 100 days of skilled care following an acute hospitalization. This is commonly available in designated beds in a nursing home.

Skilled Nursing Care

Skilled care that is administered or supervised by Registered

Nurses. Skilled nursing care can include: intravenous injections, tube feeding, and changing sterile dressings on a wound. Any service that could be safely done by an average non-medical person without the supervision of a Registered Nurse is not considered skilled care.

Skilled Nursing Facility

Also known as nursing homes, convalescent hospitals and/or rest homes, SNFs provide continuous (24-hour) nursing services (care and rehabilitation in addition to regular medical services) under a registered nurse or licensed vocational nurse. They are equipped to provide more extensive care needs, such as administering injections, monitoring blood pressure, and caring for patients on ventilators, or those requiring intravenous feeding. However, many residents in skilled nursing facilities may be receiving only "custodial" care such as help with bathing, eating, getting in and out of bed, and using the toilet. In addition,

SNFs must provide recreational activities for residents. They may also provide rehabilitative services, such as physical, occupational, or speech therapies. SNF care can be costly (an average of $40,000 per year).

Social Health Maintenance Organization

Known as SHMO, this organization provides a unique alternative to traditional HMO by combining preventive, acute and long-term care benefits. A managed system of health and long-term care services geared toward an elderly client population. Under this model, a single provider entity assumes responsibility for a full range of acute inpatient, ambulatory, rehabilitative, extended home health and personal care services under a fixed budget, which is determined prospectively. Elderly people who reside in the target service area are voluntarily enrolled. Once enrolled, individuals are obligated to receive all SHMO covered services through SHMO providers, similar to the operation of a medical model health maintenance organization.

Social Security Disability Insurance

A system (known as SSDI) of federally provided payments to eligible workers (and, in some cases, their families) when they are unable to continue working because of a disability. Benefits begin with the sixth full month of disability and continue until the individual is capable of substantial gainful activity.

Special Care Units

Designated area of a residential care facility or nursing home that cares specifically for the needs of people with Alzheimer's, head injuries, dementia, or other specific disorders.

Spend Down

Under the Medicaid program, a method by which an individual establishes Medicaid eligibility by reducing gross income through incurring medical expenses until net income (after medical expenses) meets Medicaid financial requirements. A resident spends down when he/she is no longer sufficiently covered by a third-party payer (usually Medicare) and has exhausted all personal assets. The resident then becomes eligible for Medicaid coverage.

Subacute Care

Serves patients needing complex care or rehabilitation. Subacute care (also known as transitional care) is defined as comprehensive inpatient care designed for someone who has an acute illness, injury or exacerbation of a disease process. It is goal oriented treatment rendered immediately after, or instead of, acute hospitalization to treat one or more specific active complex medical conditions or to administer one or more technically complex treatments, in the context of a person's underlying long-term conditions and overall situation. Subacute care may include long-term ventilator care or other procedures provided on a routine basis either at home or by trained staff at a skilled nursing facility. Subacute care is generally more intensive than traditional nursing facility care and less than acute care. It requires frequent (daily to weekly) recurrent patient assessment and review of the clinical course and treatment plan for a limited (several days to several months) time period until the condition is stabilized or a predetermined treatment course is completed.

Supplemental Security Income

Known as SSI, this program may provide monthly disability income for those who meet Social Security rules for disability who have limited income and resources. A public assistance program providing support for low-income aged, blind and disabled persons, established by Title XVI of the Social Security Act. SSI replaced state welfare programs for the aged, blind and disabled in since 1972, with a federally administered program, paying a monthly basic benefit nationwide of $284.30 for an individual and $426.40 for a couple in 1983. States may supplement this basic benefit amount.

T

Term Life Insurance

Provides coverage for individuals for a period of one or more years. Pays a death benefit only if individual dies during that term. It does not typically build cash value.

Third Party Notice

A policy provision that allows the policyholder name someone who the insurance company would notify if coverage were about to end because premiums haven't been paid. This individual can be a relative, friend, or professional such as a lawyer or accountant.

WORDS & PHRASES

Title III Services

Services provided to individuals 60 years of age and older which are funded under Title III of the Older Americans Act. Include: congregate and home-delivered meals, supportive services (e.g., transportation, information and referral, legal assistance, and more), in-home services (e.g., homemaker services, personal care, chore services, and more), and health promotion/disease prevention services (e.g., health screenings, exercise programs, and more).

Title XIX

Part of Medicaid, this is a federal and state-funded program of medical assistance to low-income individuals of all ages. There are income eligibility requirements for Medicaid.

Title XVIII

Part of Medicare, this is a federal health insurance program for persons age 65 and over (and certain disabled persons under age 65). Consists of 2 parts: Part A (hospital insurance) and Part B (optional medical insurance which covers physicians' services and outpatient care in part and which requires beneficiaries to pay a monthly premium).

Title XX Services

Known as Social Services Block Grant services. Grants given to states under the Social Security Act which fund limited amounts of social services for people of all ages (including some in-home services, abuse prevention services, and more). States are given wide discretion to determine the services to be provided and the groups that may be eligible for services, usually low income families and individuals.

Transfer of Assets

Transfer of a potential Medicaid recipient's money or possessions to a third party, which may be interpreted under state and federal Medicaid law as an attempt to qualify the person for Medicaid when he/she would not otherwise be eligible. Medicaid regulations govern time frames and conditions which individuals may transfer assets to others without jeopardizing Medicaid eligibility.

Transitional Care

Transitional care can be defined as that which is required to facilitate a shift from one disease stage and/or place of care to another. Also known as post-acute care or subacute care, a type of short-term care provided by many long-term care facilities and hospitals which may include rehabilitation services, specialized care for certain diseases, conditions and/or post-surgical care and other services associated with the transition between the hospital and home. Residents on these units often have been hospitalized recently and typically have more complicated medical needs. The goal of subacute care is to discharge residents to their homes or to a lower level of care.

Trust

A legal title to property held by one party for the benefit of another. An arrangement in which an individual (the trustor) gives fiduciary control of property to a person or institution (the trustee) for the benefit of one or more beneficiaries. The property so held is known as a trust.

Trustee

An individual, organization or institution (such as a bank or law firm) designated in a trust document to administer and/or manage the assets held in the trust for the benefit of the trust's beneficiary or beneficiaries.

Trustor

And individual, organization or institution (such as a bank), that holds legal title to property in order to administer it for a beneficiary

TTY

A text telephone system that allows a hearing-impaired user

to type messages (data), one character at a time, to another person and read responses on a small screen. Similar to cell phone text messaging, a "read only" conversation can exist between two people who each use the equipment. An option is having a non-hearing-impaired caller utilize This term refers to a means of sending data one character at a time. a relay service where a special operator acts as a go-between to translate the speaker's words into text and text print into voice communication.

U

Universal Life Insurance

Flexible type of policy that allows individuals to periodically adjust their premium payments and the amount of coverage.

V

Veterans Benefit Information Online

Military Records Request

http://www.archives.gov

National Cemetery Administration

http://www.cem.va.gov/

VA Facility Directory

http://www1.va.gov

Veterans Health Administration

http://www.appc1.va.gov

Veterans Benefits Administration

http://www.va.gov/

Federal Benefits For Veterans

http://www1.va.gov/opa/vadocs/Fedben.pdf

Visiting Nurse Association

A voluntary health agency that is a not-for-profit organization providing intermittent, skilled care in the home under orders from your physician. Basic services include health supervision, education and counseling; beside care; and the carrying out of physicians orders. Personnel include nurses and home health aides who are trained for specific tasks of personal bedside care. These agencies are committed to providing the finest home health care available, regardless of an individual's ability to pay.

W

Whole Life Insurance

Policies that build cash value and cover a person for as long as he or she lives if premiums continue to be paid.

PART XI
Notes

NOTES

NOTES

NOTES

NOTES

NOTES

NOTES

NOTES

NOTES

NOTES

NOTES

ABOUT THE AUTHOR

Dee Marrella has experienced life as a military wife and a corporate wife and as a result has seen much of the world and experienced many varied cultures. Born in Paterson, New Jersey, Dee spent twenty plus years in the field of education in both Europe and the United States. Experiencing these different cultures afforded her the opportunity to observe vast differences in the ways caregivers interact with both young and old individuals within societies.

In 1994 it was medically necessary for Dee's mother to enter a nursing home. Dee's constant presence at the home, watching so many caregivers deal with pain, love and guilt gave her the inspiration to create **Who Cares**.

Dee resides in Wyomissing, PA with her husband Len. They are proud parents of three grown daughters who have given them seven grandchildren.

ABOUT THE AUTHOR

NOTES

If you found this book thought provoking and

there is an interest in having the author speak to

your organization, please feel free to

contact her at:

Dee Marrella
Contact Information
(407) 688-1156
(610) 288-5801 (*fax*)
dmarrella@yahoo.com(e-mail)
www.FocusOnEthics.com